THE
ICE SKATER'S
BIBLE

Richard M. Stephenson
and
Theodore G. Clarke

1982
DOUBLEDAY & COMPANY, INC., GARDEN CITY, NEW YORK

BOOK DESIGN BY SYLVIA DEMONTE-BAYARD

Library of Congress Cataloging in Publication Data

Stephenson, Richard Montgomery, 1917–
  The ice skater's bible.

  Bibliography: p. 131.
  1. Skating.   I. Clarke, Theodore G.   II. Title.
GV849.S83   1982   796.91
AACR2
ISBN 0-385-17506-X
Library of Congress Catalog Card Number 81–43659

CONTENTS

PREFACE

This book is written primarily for beginning skaters, although some of the material will be of interest to skaters at every level as well as to those who enjoy watching them in person or on television. Since a beginner seldom knows what his or her eventual goals may be, we have started off with the fundamentals—what we believe every skater should know. Later chapters cover in more detail points of interest for those who plan to go into hockey, speed, or figure skating.

The authors would like to thank the following skaters who served as models for various movements described in the book: Robert Cook, Kenny Di Capua, Laura-Ann Edmunds, Jackie, Jeanne, and Megan Hoyt, JoEllen Krapf, Ellie and John McKey, Robert, Sara Jeanne, and Susan Powell, Lauren Showstack, Anne Spiewack, Gloria Sykes, Sara Walther, and Jim Yorke. These skaters received no pay. Our cover skaters are Jeff and Suzie Nolt. The appearance of the amateur figure skaters has been sanctioned by the United States Figure Skating Association, and the figure skating photos were taken by Anna-May Walker. Hockey photos of Robert Cook and Kenny Di Capua were taken by John Hall, who helped prepare several of the other illustrations as well. We would also like to thank the Skating Club of Boston and the University of Connecticut for the use of their ice rinks.

Others whose assistance in the preparation of this book should be acknowledged are J. A. Bosmans, of the Fries Museum, for information on the history of skating in the Netherlands; the Canadian Sport Information Resource Center, for material on Gaetan Boucher; John L. Chapman, head coach of hockey at the University of Connecticut, for his help with the fundamentals of hockey skating; J. W. Fitsell, historian and past president of the International Hockey Hall of Fame and Museum in Kingston, Ontario, for information on the origin of hockey in Canada; Charles F. Paprzyca, of Hartford, for several drawings and diagrams that help clarify the text; Andrew Pyper, for the translation of several old Dutch references; Mary Sand and Art Smith, for help with the fundamentals of speed skating; and Cynthia M. Stansfield for the use of photographs taken at the 1981 World Figure Skating Championships in Hartford, Connecticut.

Our particular thanks go to Mary Stephenson, who edited and typed the manuscript and who did the lettering for several of the illustrations.

Dick Stephenson and Ted Clarke
Storrs, Connecticut
August 23, 1981

THE
ICE SKATER'S
BIBLE

1

Introduction and History

Ice is truly a magic surface.

As you skate around your favorite rink or pond, think about what a miracle it is that we have any skating at all. The world we live in is made up of thousands of different chemical compounds, but it turns out that ordinary ice is one of the most remarkable materials we have. It is so unusual, in fact, that it is often called "the magic surface."

Probably the most remarkable property of ice is that it floats in water. The solid form of almost every other material known to chemists sinks in the liquid. If ice acted this way, it would be on the bottom of the pond—and there would be no skating.

Another remarkable property of ice is the very low friction when something is dragged across its surface. Force a skate across a wood or concrete floor, and what happens? You have to pull or push pretty hard, and it would quickly wear down the blade of the skate. Over ice, a skate blade slides easily and without damage. Not only that—the friction on ice is little different for a heavy object or a light object, so that a grown man slides over it as easily as a young child.

A third remarkable fact is that sometimes we are not even skating on the ice at all. At an indoor rink, or outdoors when the temperature is not too low, the pressure of a skate blade causes the ice directly under it to melt. We are not skating on the ice itself but on a very thin layer of water beneath the blade!

WHY DO PEOPLE SKATE?

Most of us skate purely for the fun of it—and also perhaps for enjoyable exercise in the fresh air. Skating is good exercise, particularly for the heart and lungs. It is also a good way to "unwind" after a day in school or in an office. It is something you can do all your life: you can skate as long as you can walk. You can skate alone or with friends, or it is something the entire family can do together.

You can take skating as seriously as you want. Ice skating can be divided into four categories today: recreational skating, speed skating, hockey, and figure skating. *Recreational* skating includes those people who are interested in learning only enough to feel comfortable skating around the local rink or pond on a Saturday or Sunday afternoon general skating session. They are skating just for fun and exercise. Although most of them are children, more and more adults are recognizing the value of skating and looking for places to skate. Many ice rinks now have special midweek skating sessions for housewives and also for senior citizens.

Speed skating is exactly what the name says—skating as fast as possible. Speed skating involves the use of long flat runners and is probably the oldest form of skating in existence. In comparison with the other types of skating, however, speed skating is not very popular in the United States. It requires large frozen bodies of water and is pretty much confined to regions with long cold winters, such as Wisconsin, upper Michigan, and the Adirondack area of New York State.

With the rapid growth of the professional leagues, *hockey* has become an increasingly popular form of skating in recent years. It requires quick forward movement, rapid turns, and the ability to "stop on a dime." Stick-handling is important in hockey, of course, but when you watch good hockey players, you will see that they are always good skaters. With the growing number of indoor rinks, hockey has become very popular at universities, colleges, and high schools, and more and more municipal recreation departments encourage youth and pee-wee hockey teams.

Figure skating requires precisely controlled movements on the ice, such as pivots, spins, turns, and jumps. These movements are made possible by using a specially designed curved blade. There are four distinct branches of figure skating: the compulsory (or school) figures, free skating, pair skating, and ice dancing. Figure skating has been highly developed in the United States, and the United States Figure Skating Association has member clubs located throughout the country, which conduct tests and competitions and ultimately provide the skaters who will compete in the Olympic and World championships.

THE EARLY HISTORY OF SKATING

Nobody really knows where or when skating began. The very earliest evidence of skating has been provided by the discovery throughout all of northern Europe of early bone "skates." These are simply the leg bones of animals, about a foot long, with the center hollowed out and a hole carved at one end so they could be attached with leather thongs to a sled or possibly to feet. It is most likely that they were first used as runners for a sled to draw heavy loads across the ice. It is also possible that some children of a thousand years ago (or more) tied them to their feet to play on the ice. An account of the Town of London written in 1180 states that boys would tie bones to their feet and push themselves over the ice with a pointed stick.

There is little doubt, however, that skating on a metal blade originated in the Netherlands, where the frozen canals served as winter highways. The earliest recorded mention of blade-skating is in a book published by Johannes Brugman in the year 1498. This book tells the story of St. Lydwina, who lived in the village of Schiedam near Rotterdam. A wood engraving shows her falling on the ice while skating as a young girl, an accident that apparently brought on great suffering and caused her to become completely bedridden. She bore her agony with great patience, was later beatified, and is considered to be the patron saint of skaters.

During the sixteenth and seventeenth centuries, many Dutch artists, including Hendrick Avercamp and Rembrandt, painted scenes of skaters on the ice. To the practical Dutch, skating was an important means of transportation in wintertime. Some scenes show the farmer's wife skating to market with a basket on her head. Others show in great detail townspeople or villagers gathered on the ice—men, women, and children on skates, playing games and clowning around very much as people do today. Skating had obviously become very common by this

The earliest known skating illustration, a 1498 woodcut by Johannes Brugman entitled "Vita Lidwine." (By permission of the Houghton Library, Harvard University)

"Winter Landscape with Ice Skaters," painted in the early seventeenth century by Hendrick Avercamp. (By permission of the Rijksmuseum, Amsterdam)

time and was probably the favorite winter amusement throughout all of the Netherlands.

Skating was introduced into England by the middle of the seventeenth century, probably by visiting Dutch sailors, and this led in turn to the development of a new style of skating. Interested primarily in getting from one place to another on their frozen canals, the Dutch had been using a long flat blade designed primarily for speed. The English skated mostly on small frozen ponds and began to develop a style of skating that would permit quick turns, pivots, circles, and figures on the ice. By curving the blade slightly, they made this "figuring" possible, and it soon became known as *figure* skating.

SPEED SKATING LED THE WAY . . .

Skating primarily for speed originated in the Netherlands, particularly in the northern province of Friesland where winters are colder and the canals remain frozen longer. The skate blades used by Frieslanders were longer and flatter than those used in the southern part of the Netherlands and better adapted for speed. Skating served as an important means of transportation between towns and was also the chief winter sport. The towns and the skating clubs employed "sweepers" to clear snow from the canals, to mark dangerous spots on the ice, and to erect guideposts to facilitate travel between towns. Tents and refreshment stands were located along the canals, where skaters could rest and have something to eat or drink: some bread and cheese, hot spiced milk, or a drink of the local schnapps.

It was not surprising that the Frieslanders became interested in racing. Informal skating contests date back almost as far as skating itself in this area. Clubs were formed to promote speed skating, and each town or village developed its own champions. A particular challenge was to visit in one day the eleven cities of Friesland, a circuit of some 120 miles, and a 1763 book entitled *The Present State of Friesland* notes: "It has happened more than once that good ice skaters have skated through all eleven towns of Friesland in one day; they had to keep moving fast and the ice had to be good and strong."

By the middle of the nineteenth century, speed skating had become a national sport with avid contestants and substantial prizes. In Leeuwarden, capital of Friesland, costumed ice shows and costumed races were held, and the townspeople would celebrate with flags, drums, and parades through the streets. The entire population would turn out for the races, and even today tens of thousands of spectators are not unusual at speed skating races.

In 1890, Willem Mulier made a tour of the eleven Friesland towns in 12 hours and 55 minutes. He suggested that a yearly contest be held to determine the champion of Friesland, and in 1909 the Friesland Skating Club organized the first formal *Elfstedentocht* (tour of the eleven towns). This became an annual event whenever ice and political conditions permitted, and the day of the race would be the high point of the winter season in Friesland, with hundreds of skaters entering the competition. Unfortunately, the Elfstedentocht has become a victim of modern technology, and the last race was held in 1963. Because of the industrialization of Friesland and the use of larger ships in the inland waterways, the ice does not get strong enough for this event—it has been replaced by a bicycle race in the springtime!

In 1864, the Amsterdam Ice Club was formed "to promote racing and artistic skating," and in the 1880s the Royal Netherlands Skating Club appeared. These two groups established rules for competitions and have done much to encourage and control the development of skating in the Netherlands.

A second cradle of speed skating was the Fen district of northeast England. This large region of locks and canals was originally developed by Dutch engineers, and skating had been introduced there by Dutch and Flemish workers and seamen. By the early nineteenth century, there were claimants to the title of "Champion of the Fens," and races were being held regularly during years when the winter was cold enough to provide good ice. Touring on ice, known in England as "fen-running," became popular in the middle of the nineteenth century. This involved skating journeys over long stretches of frozen lake or canal with overnight stops at villages along the way. Touring was to become even more popular in the Netherlands. Often these tours involved formidable journeys of fifty miles or more, with many skaters going along

Joseph F. Donoghue and Alex von Panschin in The Two-mile International Race at Amsterdam, January 10, 1889. (From Skating—The Badminton Library *by J. M. Heathcote, et al.)*

A fen skater. (From Handbook of Fen Skating *by Neville and Albert Goodman)*

just for fun, although the element of racing was never entirely absent. (Great Britain's National Skating Association was founded in 1879, in fact, to promote and regulate speed skating—two years later they accepted the responsibility for figure skating as well.)

FOLLOWED BY FIGURE SKATING . . .

With their well-known enthusiasm for sports and games, it was really not surprising that the English soon developed rules to cover their new sport of figure skating. The first skating textbook was written in England in 1771 by Robert Jones, a lieutenant of artillery. It describes various movements on the ice, including the inside edge, the outside edge, the spiral, the three turn, and the spread eagle, so it is obvious that figure skating was developing rapidly by that time. At about this time, also, the first skating club was founded in Edinburgh, Scotland, and London's famous Skating Club was established in 1830. This latter was a very select and exclusive organization that included a number of first-class skaters who were bringing about very rapid advancements in the art of figure skating. Various turns (three, bracket, rocker, and counter) were developed at about this time, pair skating and dancing on ice became popular as ladies were welcomed into the club, and substantial improvements were made in the design of the figure skate itself. By the end of the nineteenth century, the basic groundwork for modern figure skating had been completed.

"The Reverend William Walker Skating on Duddingston Loch," painted by Sir Henry Raeburn around the close of the eighteenth century. (By permission of the National Galleries of Scotland)

"The Skater," painted by Gilbert Stuart in 1782. (By permission of the National Gallery of Art, Washington, D.C., Andrew W. Mellon Collection)

Skating Match at Chatteris. (*From* Handbook of Fen Skating *by Neville and Albert Goodman*)

In the United States, ice skating had begun about the middle of the eighteenth century, probably introduced by British army officers stationed in the Philadelphia area. The American artist, Benjamin West, was raised near Philadelphia and is reported to have been one of that city's first notable skaters. Gilbert Stuart, a pupil of West's, came from Rhode Island and was also an expert skater. When Stuart was painting in London in 1782, arrangements were made for him to do a portrait of William Grant, a Scottish gentleman from Congalton near Edinburgh. Arriving at Stuart's studio, Grant announced that he regretted the appointment because of the excessive coldness of the weather, and he observed that the day was better suited to skating than to sitting for a portrait. Stuart agreed, and the two went out to skate on the Serpentine in Hyde Park where a number of people soon gathered to watch Stuart skate. When Stuart and Grant returned to the studio, the artist decided he would paint his subject "in the attitude of skating"—thereby creating one of the first and most famous skating scenes by an American artist.

By the start of the nineteenth century, ice skating had spread up and down the East Coast. The first club was the Philadelphia Skating Club, established in 1849 and amalgamated a few years later to form the Philadelphia Skating

Club and Humane Society (evidently falling through the ice was a real danger in the Philadelphia area). The New York Skating Club was formed in 1863 and soon became another important center for figure skating. Several of its members made important advancements in the design of the figure skate. Irving Brokaw, a successful New York businessman, went to Europe to study figure skating and helped to introduce the present-day "International" style of figure skating in the United States. His book, *The Art of Skating*, published in 1910 and widely reprinted, did much to encourage skating. In 1915, Brokaw arranged with the New York Hippodrome, America's largest theater, to bring from Berlin an ice skating comedy entitled *Flirting at St. Moritz*. Its leading skater was Charlotte Oelschlagel, one of the greatest show skaters of all time. The show was an immediate success and did much to promote figure skating in this country. Charlotte became the toast of Broadway, a "Charlotte Waltz" was composed for her, and she followed her New York appearance with a tour of the United States.

An eleven-year-old girl entered in the ladies' competition of the 1924 Olympics at Chamonix was to revolutionize figure skating. Sonja Henie, a chubby, fair-haired little girl wearing a dress that did not even reach her knees, had been en-

"Charlotte" and *Irving Brokaw in pair skating spiral.* (*From* Hippodrome Skating Book *by* Charlotte [Oelschlagel])

tered in the championship "to gain experience." Her performance was based on vigorous athletic skating rather than on the purely graceful movements that had characterized figure skating up to that time. Although Sonja finished last in the competition, one far-seeing judge placed her first in the free skating. Less than three years later, she was world champion.

Sonja Henie made tremendous contributions to figure skating. She attracted large crowds wherever she competed. Skating suddenly became more athletic as women replaced their ankle-length skirts and wide hats with more appropriate skating costumes. After winning ten world championships, Sonja retired from amateur competition in 1936 to join the professional ranks. She starred in an ice skating show that toured the United States to enthusiastic packed houses. When her tour was completed, Sonja Henie went to Hollywood and rented the only ice rink there to put on her own show. A few months later, she was the star of the first great skating film, *One in a Million,* and she went on to star in ten more films before leaving Hollywood. Skating films appeared in movie houses across America, and public interest in figure skating mushroomed everywhere. Touring ice shows such as Ice Capades and Holiday on Ice began crisscrossing the country.

AND HOCKEY

Games on the ice are as old as skating itself. Sixteenth- and seventeenth-century Dutch paintings clearly show grown men—sometimes alone and sometimes in groups—hitting a ball

"Enjoying the Ice," painted around the mid-seventeenth century by Barent Avercamp. (By permission of the Rijksmuseum, Amsterdam)

on the ice with bent sticks. This was a game similar to croquet, since the object was to hit a vertical post in the ice. The bent stick used to strike the ball was known as a *kolf,* and some historians believe this may have been a forerunner of the game of golf. There is no evidence that this early Dutch game bore any direct relationship to ice hockey, and the sharp-eyed observer will note that in most of these paintings the players are not even wearing skates. Even today, hockey is not an important sport in the Netherlands.

Field hockey, of course, had been known in England since medieval times in one form or another. Its most primitive form, called *shinny* or *shinty,* was often played down the middle of a village street by boys armed with bent sticks who would knock a "cat" around in a rough-

and-tumble game, all against all. Sometimes sides were chosen, and it would become more recognizable as a game—with hedges perhaps marking side boundaries and a couple of stones to mark the goals. Gradually this game acquired respectability, formal rules were established, and the formation of the Wimbledon Hockey Club in 1883 gave it the badge of gentility. A game of the same type played in Ireland is known as *hurley* and in Scotland as *shinty.*

With field hockey being played during the warmer months to serve as a guide, it was inevitable that a similar game would sooner or later be established on ice. Known as *bandy* or *hockey-on-ice,* the first organized game appeared in the Fen district of England. The bandy was a curved stick, usually cut from the lower branches of willow trees that grew along

"Dribbling at Bandy." (*From* Skating—The Badminton Library *by J. M. Heathcote, et al.*)

the fens. The *cat* or *kit* was usually a ball (sometimes a cricket ball, later an India rubber ball) but a bung of wood or cork often sufficed. There is little doubt that bandy was played in the eighteenth century in the fens, but the first recorded evidence shows that games were played in Bury Fen during the great frost of 1813–14. In 1882, formal rules were established by the Blutisham and Earith Skating Hockey Club. There were to be fifteen players on a side, the goals were to be 22 feet wide and located 220 yards apart, and the India rubber ball was to be 2½ inches in diameter. A player could raise his bandy no higher than his shoulder, and any tripping or rough play was to be "peremptorily put down by the Umpire or Captains." If a player threw or dropped his bandy, an opponent could pick it up and throw it away!

Following formation of the National Skating Association in 1879, bandy was played in and around London for a time. In an attempt to widen interest in the game, members of the Bury Fen team played exhibition matches in the

Netherlands, but these attempts were unsuccessful, and bandy gradually faded out—to be replaced by the modern game of ice hockey.

Modern ice hockey first appeared in Canada, where long winters and many lakes made games on ice a natural winter sport. The game was probably first introduced by British soldiers and sailors stationed in Canada who tied skates to their boots and knocked a ball around the ice in a bandy-like diversion. English troops were stationed in Kingston from 1783 to 1855, and it is known that they played field hockey and that many of them were proficient skaters. There is evidence that soldiers in Kingston played shinny on the harbor ice in the 1850s, and that shinty was played on skates in Ottawa in 1852 and "hockey" on the inner harbor of Halifax in 1851. From this, the game quickly spread to civilians. The modern game came about as the result of three major changes: (1) substitution of the hockey puck for the ball; (2) use of a hockey net to replace the two posts as goals; and (3) the establishment of modern rules, which re-

"The Victoria Hockey Club, 1888." (*By permission of Notman Photographic Archives, McCord Museum, McGill University, Montreal*)

duced the size of the rink and the number of players to those we know today.

According to J. W. Fitsell, historian of the International Hockey Hall of Fame and Museum in Kingston, Ontario, a puck was used in the game of hockey in Montreal in the 1870s. A flat circular piece of wood was used in the first recorded game in that city in 1875, and the word *puck* was used in the following year. Pioneers of the game in Montreal are quoted as saying that the first pucks made of rubber were two-inch cubes. In 1886, a description of the puck published in Montreal when the Dominion Hockey Association was formed read: "One inch thick and three inches in diameter." That is the same year in which the first organized game was played in Kingston with a cut-down lacrosse ball. This irregularly shaped puck is on display in the Kingston museum and is the oldest puck known to exist today.

The first hockey games in Montreal were played at the Victoria Rink, the best indoor rink

in the world at that time. It is interesting to note that the ice surface, 85 by 200 feet, was precisely the same as is used today. Flags were used to mark the two 8-foot-wide goals. The earliest games were played with nine players on a side, but by 1877 this had been reduced to eight on a side.

The original rules of the Canadian game of ice hockey were published in Montreal in 1877. The game was begun with "a bully in the centre of the ground" (*bully* was a term taken from field hockey and referred to a primitive face-off). The *on-side* rule was also taken from field hockey: "A player must always be on his own side of the ball . . ." Players were referred to as "gentlemen," and it was made clear that "charging from behind, tripping, collaring, kicking, or shinning shall not be allowed."

Hockey developed rapidly throughout all of Canada during the final two decades of the nineteenth century. Covered rinks were found in practically every city or good-sized town. Stu-

A hockey match at the Victoria Rink in 1893. (By permission of Notman Photographic Archives, McCord Museum, McGill University, Montreal)

dents at McGill University in Montreal adopted the sport in 1877, and—together with groups such as the Victoria Hockey Club and the Ontario Hockey Association—they gradually modified the rules of the game. Goals were narrowed to six feet in width with a crossbar four feet off the ice. Teams were reduced to seven players (later six), and the size of the stick blade was defined. Play was allowed behind the goals (in contrast to bandy and field hockey, where a ball hit behind the goal line was a *bye*, and the goalkeeper was allowed a free hit). In 1892, Lord Stanley, then governor-general of Canada, donated the Stanley Cup as a symbol of hockey supremacy. This effectively marked the beginning of the game as we know it today.

The years following the Second World War witnessed a spectacular growth in sports and recreational activity of all kinds in the United States. Construction of many new artificial ice rinks caused increased interest in figure skating, hockey, and recreational skating. The United States had its first figure skating gold medal when a young athletic skater from Harvard, Dick Button, won the men's championship at the 1948 winter Olympics. Figure skating became popular in places such as Southern California where there is no natural ice. More and more universities, colleges, high schools, and prep schools became interested in hockey. The National Hockey League, which for years had consisted of only six teams, expanded to twenty-one teams distributed throughout the United States and Canada. At the 1980 winter Olympics, Americans proudly applauded the success of our amateur hockey team and the racing performances of Eric and Beth Heiden. Ice skating had come a long way since children first tied bones on their feet to slide over the ice some thousand years ago.

2

Equipment and Clothing

The first decision that faces someone planning to skate is obviously the proper selection of a pair of skates. (To the expert, *skate* means the blade only, but most people in the United States refer to the combination of boot and blade as the skate.) You will find that there are four types of skates available in a sporting-goods store: double-runners, racing skates, figure skates, and hockey skates. What is the best choice for a beginner?

Double-runners are sometimes purchased for very young children. They do not glide on the ice, and when the ice is hard they will not dig in, so that the child simply slips around on the surface of the ice. It is quite impossible for a child to learn even the most basic principles of balance on double-runners. Besides, children who start out on double-runners will often resist being put on single blades. What we are saying,

then, is that double-runners are a waste of money and should never be used at all.

Racing skates are very tricky to handle and require considerable skating skill. They are not suitable for beginners. In addition, many ice rinks will not permit their use because of the potential danger of their long blades to other skaters in the event of a fall.

The choice for the beginner of any age really boils down to a decision between figure skates and hockey skates. In the past, it was commonly assumed that girls were primarily interested in figure skates and boys in hockey skates. Today, although many girls are interested in hockey and speed skating and boys are showing a growing interest in figure skating, many teachers believe it is a good idea for all children to begin on figure skates. Because the figure blade is lower than the hockey blade and the figure skating boot comes up higher on the ankle, well-fitted figure skates provide better support than hockey skates. Also, the basic skating movements are easier to learn on figure skates and can be easily carried over to hockey or racing skates later. Once skating is learned on hockey skates, the change to figure skates is somewhat difficult. Moreover, it should not be assumed that all beginners are children; more and more adults are interested in skating today—many for the first time—and in almost every instance they are finding figure skates easier to use.

YOUR FIRST FIGURE SKATES

Medium-priced figure skates are usually sold with the boot and blade either riveted or screwed together as a unit. In the better figure skates, the blade and the boot are sold separately, and the blade is then attached to the boot with ordinary screws. The first and most important matter for consideration, however, is the fit of the boot. Normally, figure skating boots are a half size *smaller* (never larger) than the ordinary walking shoe, and they should always be fitted over thin socks or tights. One or more layers of thick wool socks will lessen the support provided by the boots. They do *not* keep the feet any warmer because without a

good fit the boots must be very tightly laced in order to have any kind of support—and this tends to cut off the circulation.

A well-fitted skating boot will be snug around the instep and particularly around the heel. When trying on a properly laced skating boot, have someone hold the blade down and try to lift your heel from the bottom of the boot. If it slides up and down, the heel of the boot may be too large for you. If you wear medium-width walking shoes, you will probably have no trouble getting a good fit in a stock boot; however, if you have particularly wide or narrow feet, you may have to go to the more expensive boots, which come in narrow and wide widths. The heel must be snug, there must not be much buckling of the leather around the ankle, and there should be a gap of one or one and a half inches between the lacings over the instep. Traditionally, girls have worn white figure skating boots and boys black, but the fit of the boot is far more important than its color. You should be prepared to spend several sessions breaking in a pair of new boots; more experienced skaters usually bring along their old skates and change off for a few times to avoid blisters that might keep them off the ice for a day or two.

While less important than the boots, the figure skating blades should be of fairly good quality steel or they will need frequent sharpening. Figure blades are normally curved from front to back on a six-foot radius or *rocker* that permits easy turns on the ice. In addition, each blade is hollow-ground to give it an *inside edge* (the edge on the inside of the foot) and an *outside edge* (the edge on the outside of the foot). For an experienced figure skater, the grinding or sharpening of the blades is a serious business, since a poor sharpening job can flatten the blades and ruin them in no time at all. Rather than trust your skates to the local hardware store, it is better to ask a good figure skater where he or she has skates sharpened. Even if the sharpening itself costs more, your blades will last far longer and you will enjoy skating much more when it is well done.

Those sharp spikes at the front of a figure blade are known as the *toe picks* or *toe rakes*. They are used in certain jumps and spins but not for ordinary stroking around the rink. Beginners frequently catch the toe picks on the ice, which can lead to unpleasant falls—often on the

A figure skate.

A figure skating blade with rocker exaggerated to illustrate curvature.

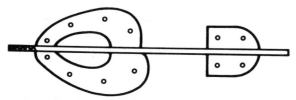

View of figure skating blade showing the screw holes.

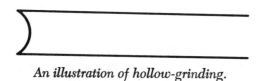

An illustration of hollow-grinding.

knees. This happens when the foot is not held at the proper angle for stroking; in other words, the toe picks actually force a beginner to learn proper care in stroking—"the hard way." Some beginners have the lowest toe pick ground down a bit or even removed, but this also removes the need to develop proper stroking technique and is not a good idea.

Another word of warning: Many parents tend to buy the cheapest skates they can find for a child's first pair, often a size or two larger than the child's present shoe size to allow "room to grow in." This is a mistake. No child can learn or enjoy skating in boots so large or so poorly constructed that they provide no support. We've all seen so-called "weak ankles" that practically flop on the ice. The fact is that many children are so turned off by this experience that they give up and think skating is not for them. For the parent concerned about whether or not a child will really *like* skating, it is wiser to rent skates for the first few times to see how it goes. Even rented skates should be fitted as well as possible, and this is also true of hand-me-downs. Some dealers will allow skates to be traded in on a new pair, and there is a ready market at any rink for secondhand skates in reasonably

good condition. You will find that it is usually less costly in the long run to buy a pair of good well-fitted skates that can be sold later at a fair price than to buy junk that has to be just thrown out eventually.

For an adult, of course, there is no real problem about buying skates. Rent a pair for the first few times on the ice. When you decide you like skating, buy the very best pair you can afford. If you keep in mind these basic rules for fit, they will with reasonable care give you much pleasure and last the rest of your life.

SETTING THE BLADES

Even if your first boots come with blades already attached, it is important to be sure that the blades are located in the correct position on the soles of the boots. In order to offset the natural tendency of ankles to turn inward—and to make it easier for the skater to get on an outside edge—figure blades are not mounted directly in the center of the boot but rather are set slightly to the inside of the centerline. You will find that

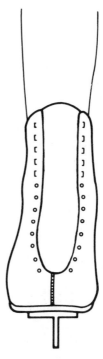

A figure skate with blade set slightly to the inside of the centerline.

new blades are often attached with only five or six screws, so that you can try them out for a while. If you are not comfortable, it is still possible to remove the screws, plug the holes, make new screw holes, and adjust the blades to a new setting. These adjustments should be made under the supervision of someone with experience—don't try to do it yourself at first.

When blades are riveted to the boots, however, it is impossible to correct the setting. If you buy blades and boots that come as a unit, we recommend that you check first to see whether the blades are riveted or screwed to the boots, and then where the blades are mounted. Cheap skates sometimes have the blades placed *outside* the centerline, and this will make skating very difficult.

A hockey skate.

LACING THE BOOTS

It is extremely important to lace up figure skating boots properly, and even young children should be taught this as soon as possible. Many a first-time skater comes off the ice after a short while complaining of "weak ankles" or leg cramps—when the only problem is poor lacing of the boots.

To begin with, put on your skates and make sure your socks are pulled up all the way; wrinkled socks are uncomfortable and can cause blisters. Make sure also that the tongue of the boot is centered and pulled all the way up. Start tightening the laces beginning from the toe. The first three or four eyelets must be fairly loose to avoid cramping the toes, but the laces over the instep of your foot should be tight to give good support. Some skaters tie a loop or a surgeon's knot (hold one lace still and pass the other under it twice) at the last eyelet below the hooks to keep this part of the boot very snug. From there to the top of the boot, the lacing should be fairly loose so that the top of the ankle turns easily and there is no binding at the top of the boot. Many skaters do not use the two top hooks at all. In any case, be sure that your laces are well tied and cannot come loose to trip you on the ice.

Most skaters today use nylon laces, since they are thinner and stronger than cotton. On the other hand, nylon laces have more *give* to them. Some advanced skaters prefer cotton because it is less likely to stretch during competitions. It is always a good idea to carry an extra pair of laces. You never know when a lace will break, and new ones in the proper length are not always available to buy when you need them.

HOCKEY SKATES

Hockey skates differ from figure skates in several ways. They are set higher off the ice (that is, they have more *rise*) to permit sharper bending of the foot during sudden stops and turns. The blades are thinner, much flatter than figure blades, and always permanently attached to the boots. Hockey blades are usually ground pretty much flat across, with little or no hollow grinding. There are no toe picks, and the back of the hockey blade is rounded or may have a small plastic cap to minimize the possibility of injury during falls.

If anything, hockey players are even more particular about their skates than figure skaters! The three forwards are continually stopping and starting, so they prefer a shorter blade with a slight rocker. The two defensemen do more turning and backward skating, so they want more blade on the ice and a slightly longer blade with less rocker. For stopping the puck (*skate saves*), the goalie requires long blades that are completely flat with no rocker at all. Hockey blades are often set on the outside of the centerline to facilitate getting on the inside edge for powerful stops and starts. The hockey boot is thicker, less pliable than the figure boot, and often has a plastic lining. It has a strong arch support and is well protected on the sides, particularly around the toe and heel, to prevent injury from hockey sticks or fast pucks. The back of the boot is higher than the front to provide protection for the Achilles tendon.

RACING SKATES

Racing or speed skates are designed with only one thing in mind: to go as fast as possible. The blade is long and thin, and its front end extends well beyond the toe of the boot instead of being directly attached to the boot by a stanchion, as is the case with figure and hockey skates.

Two types of racing skates are used today. *Indoor* skates are used for a 100-meter oval track (which presents an almost continuous curve), and *outdoor* skates are used for the standard 400-meter oval track (which involves alternate curves and straightaways). Speed skaters always go in a counterclockwise direction—that is, all curves travel to the left.

Outdoor skates come from Norway, Japan, and the Netherlands. The racing blade is set closer to the ice than the hockey skate (less rise). Outdoor blades are placed directly in the center of the sole, and there is a very slight rocker—only about a twenty-meter radius. The outdoor boot is low, reaching only to the ankle bone (slightly higher than ordinary oxford-style walking shoes). Most indoor skates are made in Japan. They are designed for almost continuous

skating to the left. The indoor boot is about three quarters of an inch higher than the outdoor boot to provide more support on curves, and its accompanying blade has about a five-meter rocker, four times that of the outdoor blade. To facilitate the almost continuous left turning, the indoor blade is set on the extreme left of the right boot; it is also set somewhat to the left of center on the left boot, but the position is not as extreme. Both indoor and outdoor racing blades are ground flat across, using oilstone and hand grinding. There is no hollow-grinding.

Better racing skates are presently available from only one distributor in the United States: Don Zordani, Sportif Importer, Ltd., 5225 West Lawrence Avenue, Chicago, Illinois 60630.

CARE OF BOOTS AND BLADES

With reasonable care, a good pair of skates should last you for many years. The most important consideration in the care of blades is to avoid walking on metal or concrete without *skate guards*. While most ice rinks have rubber or wood flooring in dressing rooms and around the ice itself, some caution is still needed; much sand and dirt is carried in on shoes, and this can damage blades very quickly. Skate guards are made of rubber, plastic, or wood and are worn by the more experienced skaters whenever they are off the ice. When available, wooden guards have the special advantage of making a clicking noise when you walk on them. This lessens the possibility of absent-mindedly stepping onto the ice while wearing guards, which almost inevitably results in a very spectacular fall on the ice—humorous for spectators when there is no injury, but failure to remove skate guards has caused fatal head injuries.

Children often have no idea of the damage they can do to their skates by walking on hard surfaces. Many of them put their skates on at home and then walk from the parking lot to the rink with unprotected blades! If you look closely at blades that have been badly treated, you will see completely worn-down edges and deep nicks and scratches in the metal. The blades will no longer dig into the ice properly, there is no "flow" over the ice surface, and most of the fun of skating is spoiled by this careless treatment.

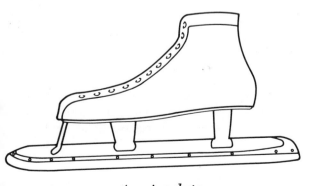

A racing skate.

The life of a pair of blades depends almost entirely on how often they must be sharpened. Skating tends to wear down the center of the blade, so that each sharpening reduces the curve of the rocker. Figure blades eventually become so flattened that they resemble hockey blades; turns become difficult or impossible, and the blades must be replaced.

Another important consideration in the care of blades is to avoid rusting. Carefully wipe them dry with a clean cloth (some skaters recommend a chamois) before you put them away. Never put them away with the guards on, since this will surely cause rusting. Allow the skates to warm gradually to room temperature—*never* put the cold blades near a heater or radiator, since this may distort them as a result of sudden thermal expansion.

If the blades are screwed to the boots, it is wise to check the tightness of the screws from time to time, particularly when the skates are new. This is a precaution that will prevent accidents caused by blades suddenly coming loose on the ice. A loose screw may also permit moisture to penetrate and cause rusting and deterioration of the screw itself. More experienced skaters often carry a screwdriver in their skate bags, and it is wise to carry extra screws and even a few toothpicks, which can be used temporarily to fill a screw hole that has "lost its threads."

The chief problem in caring for your skating boots is to protect them from sudden temperature changes and from moisture. The soles of the boots are usually painted with a waterproofing material before the blades are attached. The uppers should be cleaned each season by washing them with saddle soap; this will make the leather more flexible and tends to prevent moisture from attacking the leather. For best all-around care of your boots, we recommend monthly use of a liquid cream polish—along with plenty of elbow grease. The clear liquid polishes are easier to use but will eventually cause the leather to crack. White boots can be a special problem, since almost all white polishes merely coat the surface and do nothing to protect the leather.

WHAT TO WEAR

All clothing worn for skating should be functional. It should in no way hinder the vision of the skater, should offer some protection in case of a fall, and should be fairly close-fitting to avoid entanglement with the skates. It should be sturdy, comfortable, warm (but not too warm), light (never bulky), and should allow maximum freedom of movement. Skating is a sport, and attractive informal clothing will make you feel more at ease. Garish or offbeat outfits are out of place.

Very young children will be most comfortable in waterproof snowsuits "until they can remain on their feet longer than on their seat." Boys are usually dressed in sturdy trousers with sweaters or hip-length jackets, girls in sweaters and slacks or jeans. Parkas are not good because they restrict vision. While jeans are very popular with the teen-agers and the college crowd, they should fit comfortably. It is also important that slacks and jeans not be too loose at the ankles or too long—a bad fall can result if they get in the way of the skates. Waterproof gloves or mittens should always be worn to protect the hands in case of a fall.

For indoor skating, any informal clothing supplemented by a light sweater is the rule for beginners. Figure skating clubs often have their own dress rules. For men, a jacket and tie are sometimes worn for dancing and for club sessions. Dark colors, but not black, are customary. Thin gloves can be worn to protect the hands. Hats are not usually worn in indoor rinks, although a trim beret is seen occasionally. Women may choose to wear a short skirt with a blouse and sweater or jacket. It should have a natural waistline, a moderately high neckline, long fitted sleeves, and provide freedom of movement—particularly under the arms. Stretch fabrics are now commonly used for skating costumes. Tights are worn for warmth and protection with the short skirts. Jewelry is neither appropriate nor safe on the ice.

If you appear in a skating exhibition or an ice show, remember that simplicity and neatness of dress are of prime importance. Solid or deep colors are best, with matching or contrasting colors for accessories. Avoid pale or muddy colors or busy prints. Pale blues and greens are poor because they blend into the color of the ice. Remember that colors change with lighting, particularly when mercury-vapor lamps are used.

On a cold and windy outdoor pond or rink, of course, you will wear whatever will keep you warm, such as thermal underwear or long johns. For hockey and racing skaters, the costume is highly specialized as you become more and more proficient—this will be described in more detail in Chapters 6 and 7.

3

Your First Time on the Ice

When you first go to an ice rink, it might be a good idea just to watch for a little while to get a feeling for the atmosphere of the place: watch the skaters enjoying themselves, feel the tempo of movement on the ice, pick out some good skaters and watch what they are doing. When you are ready to get out on the ice yourself, be sure your skates are laced the way we described in Chapter 2, and also be sure the lacings are secure and tucked in. Before you step on the ice, remove your guards and put them where you can find them later.

Step onto the ice carefully, somewhat the way you test the water before going into a swimming pool. Hold onto the side of the rink (the barrier), and step sideways onto the ice surface one foot at a time. Get clear of the entrance with the help of a friend or by pulling yourself along the barrier to a quiet spot on the ice where you can try out your skates.

Stand motionless now for a moment to get the feel of your skate blades. Keep your body straight. Your head should be up, back straight, knees slightly bent, and feet a few inches apart. Your arms should be relaxed but held out to the sides at about waist height for balance. Holding onto the barrier or your friend, put your weight on one foot and turn the blade of the other foot on the ice—first to the inside and then to the outside—so that you can really feel each *edge*. Do the same with the other foot. Whatever you do on figure skates, you will need to keep the erect posture you have just learned.

Now you're ready to move. Most beginners try to *walk* on the ice. This is not correct, but it won't be harmful at this point if you take very short steps. Whether you use a walking motion to get yourself going or pull yourself along the barrier with one hand, or have a friend (or two) help you along, you need first of all to get the feeling of gliding forward on the ice. For correct balance in forward skating, your weight should be just slightly back of the center of the blade. (Take the time to feel this, because transferring your weight forward to the toe picks can result in very sudden contact with the ice—on your knees!) Take a few short steps, put your feet together, and *glide*. Your ankles should be straight. This is not always easy at first, but if your skates fit and are well laced and your posture is straight, there should be no problem. Your knees should be bent far enough so that you couldn't see your toes if you looked (but, of course, your head is up).

As you begin to relax and feel balanced on your forward glide, try shifting your weight from the center of your body (over both feet) to one side (over one foot). Lift the other foot just slightly and hold it close beside the other as you glide. Try this a few times on each foot. Don't think about edges at this point—for now you are gliding only on the flat part of your blades. Take it slow and easy. It's better to get these first things right than to rush ahead and develop bad habits that will be difficult to change. In Chapter 4, you will really begin to *skate*.

Getting the feel of the ice.

FALLING

Fear of falling on the ice is a problem for most beginners, particularly adults, and it can make learning to skate more difficult for you. To begin with, you *will* fall. It happens to everyone, from beginner to Olympic champion. No one is going to laugh at you, because it happens to all of us. A fall on the ice is seldom serious, since ice does have a little more give to it than our usual walking surfaces, and it also has a smooth surface that allows your momentum to continue. If you can relax your body as you fall, you will minimize the chances of serious injury. The idea is just to go limp all over and *sink* into the ice. Let's try a few falls.

First, a forward fall: While standing still, bend into a crouching position with your hands on the ice in front of you. Slide your hands forward and straighten your knees. Keep your head and chin up and allow yourself to stretch out on the ice, so that the impact is taken by your

hands (this is why gloves are needed) and your upper body. It's important to remember two things—get your hands down first to break the fall, and keep your head up.

To get up, plant yourself on both knees, place one skate on the ice and then the other—with the heels pointed at each other. Use your hands and arms then to raise yourself. If you use only your hands, you are likely to slip. If you have fallen as a result of going on the ice with your guards on, be sure to remove them before you try to get up.

Now for a backward fall: Again in a crouched position, go back on the heels of your blades, and sit down. Just let your skates go forward from under you. Keep your chin tucked into your chest and your arms up—in a backward fall, it's better not to try to get your hands down first and you will prevent a whiplash injury by tucking your head.

A forward fall.

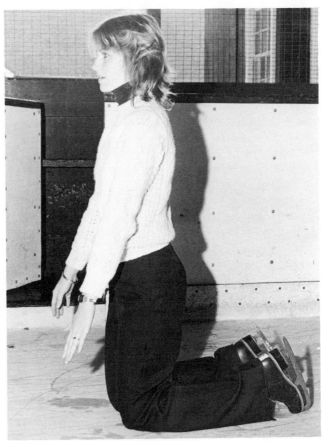

Getting up again.

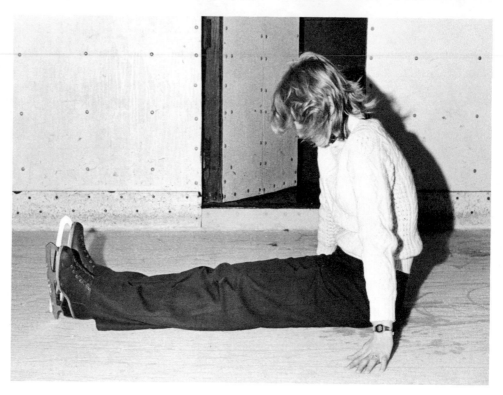

A backward fall.

In any fall you are likely to slide along the ice. When the ice is wet, you will slide farther and faster. To prevent sliding into the barrier or another person, try to dig the heel or toe of your skate blade into the ice. Get your hands up off the ice quickly, so they will not be run over by oncoming skaters.

Remember to *go limp* in a fall. Don't fight it by grabbing someone near you, and don't flail your arms about. You will probably have help, but get up as quickly as possible—and once you are up, get out of the way!

SAFETY ON THE ICE

Skating is fun and safe as long as a few "ice manners" are observed. Before you step onto the ice, always take a look to be sure you are not stepping out in front of someone. Skate near the barrier until you pick up sufficient speed to blend with the other skaters. Never cross in front of fast-moving "traffic." These few rules should be taught to children in particular, but many adults overlook them at first.

Your head should always be up, your eyes open, and your ears alert. You can avoid many accidents if you know who is around you, and what ice space you have to work with. No matter how skillful you become on the ice, if you don't see a problem developing you won't be able to avoid it.

Obviously, fooling and pushing your friends as well as weaving and cutting in between skaters can be dangerous. Stay back a bit from the person in front of you (just as you avoid tail-gating when you drive), so that a sudden swerve or fall won't find you literally on top of him or her.

Beginners tend to have a fear of anyone skating very close to them. They will often panic and move in an unexpected direction—even though an experienced skater would ordinarily have no difficulty in avoiding them. While you are a beginner, then, it is wise to stay out of the way of the better skaters when you can. The center of the ice is traditionally reserved for spinning and for people taking lessons or practicing figures. If you skate into this area where the advanced skaters are practicing, you should not expect them to watch out for you—they tend to regard this as their special province.

When you see someone having a lesson or skating to a piece of music, it will always be easier for you, the beginner, to stay clear. This could be a skater practicing a free skating program or dancers skating to dance music, and they have certain patterns to follow on the ice. You will probably enjoy watching them, and you may well be in their position someday—and appreciate this courtesy.

Skating on an ice surface with many others is similar to driving a car on a crowded highway. If anyone stops abruptly or moves too fast or too slowly, it causes problems for the rest. If you keep your eyes open and remain alert to what is going on around you, you will be able to avoid most collisions as well as angry feelings, and you and your new neighbors on the ice will enjoy this wonderful sport.

STARTER PROGRAMS

At this point, any help you can get in the way of instruction from a professional or a friend who is actively involved in figure skating will make all this easier for you. You will probably want to skate in public sessions until you feel comfortable and fairly skilled on your skates. You should learn to enjoy skating before becoming involved with figures, dancing, hockey, or speed skating instruction.

Group classes are often a good way to get in some ice time plus instruction in the basics for a minimal cost. For recreational or figure skating, there are classes that follow a regular progression of skills for beginners and intermediate skaters. These are organized at most rinks around programs set up by the United States Figure Skating Association (USFSA) or the Canadian Figure Skating Association (CFSA). The Ice Skating Institute of America (ISIA) also has programs, and there are some set up by individual ice rinks. Even if your primary interest is figure skating, you will not be ready for most club sessions for a while. These are relatively expensive and not worth the cost until you can participate more fully in their activities. If you are primarily interested in power skating or hockey, you may wish to join a power skating class or attend a hockey clinic as soon as you are skating easily. In any case, the following chapters will give you an idea of what to expect from your new sport.

4

Forward Skating—and Some Stops

Ask any advanced skater what is the most important thing to learn in becoming a good skater, and the answer will probably be "Balance!" This means more than the natural balance that has made it possible for you to stand up on your skates and glide forward comfortably. It means having your weight properly aligned—being in perfect balance—at all times, regardless of your movement or position on the ice. You'll be working toward it at every level of your skating progress, and it will make possible that first effortless glide as well as good stops, perfect circles, and all other special moves. It is the key to real confidence and joy in skating, and it comes a little at a time.

As a beginner, you should be thinking now about the correct balance point over your blades for skating forward—just back of the center of your blades. Besides centering your weight at

this point, you must hold your body weight in a direct line from head to toe. This means a straight body except for the knees, which will be bent much of the time. *Your head is up, back straight, hips tucked under your body, shoulders relaxed, and arms extended with your hands palms down at about waist height.*

SCULLING

We'll begin with a forward movement on both feet known as *sculling*. With your body positioned as we have just described, knees bent, both feet on the ice about six inches apart and your weight evenly distributed between them, point your toes outward and bring your heels together. Now your weight will be on the inside of your feet (that is, on the inside edges of your

T-position.

A one-foot glide.

blades). If you apply an even amount of pressure to the inside edge of both skates, they will begin to move apart—and your knees will straighten slightly. When the blades are about as far apart as the width of your shoulders, turn your toes *in* and bring your feet back to a parallel position about six inches apart. As they come together, increase your knee bend and flatten the blades on the ice. Point your toes out again, and repeat the entire action. Be sure you feel the inside edge of your blades gripping the ice. The power comes from the bending of your knees, not from an effort of your thigh muscles. The wider you can spread your feet (with comfort), the more speed you will gain.

STROKING

When your sculling moves right along, you are ready to learn *stroking*—that is, the action that will move you over the ice in a series of glides alternating from one foot to the other. Since the actual propulsion comes from the inside of the blade that is *leaving* the ice, the first part of a stroke is a push-off.

We are going to stroke first on the right foot. With your feet in a *T-position* (the heel of the right foot at a right angle to the instep of the left foot), anchor the inside edge of your left blade in the ice. Balance your weight over the arch of the left foot, and give your knees a slight extra bend. Now straighten the left knee (allowing the right knee to remain bent), and transfer your weight to the right foot. The left blade

Transfer of weight.

Pushing off.

should turn so that you move away from the *whole side* of the blade. You will begin to glide forward on the right foot. For now, you will be gliding in a straight line with your shoulders and hips held square to your *skating* blade in what is called *neutral position*. Your *free* leg (the one that is now off the ice) is held in back, in line with your body.

You will notice a tendency for your shoulders to swing to the side; this can be fought by keeping your skating blade erect and your hips and shoulders square. If you like, you can place your left arm slightly forward. Your skating ankle should be upright with the kneecap out beyond the toe of the blade and pointing in the direction of travel. As you know, your balance should be just back of the center of the blade.

After a short glide, you will lose speed and/or

balance, and you can bring your feet together. As you bring the left foot under you, the right knee should straighten to allow the blade of the left foot to clear the ice—try to bring this foot in *flat*, so that the toe pick won't catch on the ice. As your feet come together, turn the right foot out to 45 degrees, catch the inside edge on the ice, and let the weight transfer evenly to your left foot as you push off with the whole side of the right blade.

At first, you should not push actively with the foot that is leaving the ice—just let it leave the ice smoothly. (As you become used to the stroking action, think of pushing *down* with the inside of the blade to give you thrust.)

Always remember to keep your arms level, your knees bent, and your body straight. As your free leg moves behind you, try to turn the

A two-foot snowplow stop.

A one-foot snowplow stop.

toe out and down and keep the leg straight. Bring your feet as close to each other as you can in the transition. Be sure you do not use your toe pick to push off—this is ineffective and, in figure skating, is considered a major error. Now is the time to form your good habits!

You can lengthen your strokes and learn a smoother technique through improved timing of the knee bend and push and also through a refining of balance and body positions. The upper body must be made to do your bidding; your upper body should move very little while you are skating—and only when you choose. Overcome a tendency to bend forward as you stroke. Always keep your back straight. As your skating improves, continue to practice your stroking at the start of each session. Learn when to relax and when to push.

STOPPING IS IMPORTANT, TOO!

Skates do have brakes, but you have to learn to use them. They are the edges of your blades, and they can be used to create friction or drag and bring you skidding neatly to a stop. The feeling you want to achieve is one of scraping or lightly shaving the surface of the ice. Try this while standing at the barrier, tilting one blade and then the other so that the edge scrapes the ice. Try it while moving, too, scraping the blade at right angles to your direction of travel. Gradually increase the speed at which you do this—and then try some of the basic stops below.

THE SNOWPLOW STOP

This stop takes its name from the image of a snowplow piling snow up in front of its blade.

A hockey stop.

A T-stop.

The common snowplow stop is done by bending the knees while doing a two-foot glide, then pushing the feet apart with toes in and heels out and applying firm and even pressure so that the inside edges of your blades shave the ice. You can vary the angle of the blades until you are quite comfortable with your snowplow stop. Snowplows can also be done with only one foot scraping, the other traveling straight ahead, but this should be learned with each foot doing the stopping.

THE HOCKEY STOP

This stop is easy to explain and actually easy to do. It does require some confidence, however, since it can't be done in half measure. You simply do it, abruptly. For that reason, it is the best

emergency stop—and the one that ought to be learned by every skater.

You can learn the *feel* of this stop while holding onto the barrier. With feet pointed straight ahead and slightly apart, and with knees bent, twist your lower body sharply to the left, turning your hips, knees, and feet simultaneously. *Your shoulders remain facing squarely ahead.* As you turn to the left, keep your feet together, lower your left hip and shoulder, and release your weight by rising up on your knees and shifting your weight to the front of the blades. Return your weight to the balls of your feet as you stop, and hold your ankles straight.

The hockey stop should be learned in both directions, so you must convert what you have learned in one direction to the opposite. To do this, simply turn to the right instead of to the left, while lowering your right hip and shoulder. This type of analysis is necessary with any move being learned in two directions and can be very helpful to your learning both versions.

THE T-STOP

As its name suggests, this stop is done in the T-position with one foot skating straight ahead on the flat of the blade while the other is held at right angles to it—the instep of the back foot against the heel of the forward foot. Arms are out to the sides, shoulders square. This time you will use the *outside* edge of the back skate to stop. Shift your weight gradually to the middle of the back blade to stop. Be sure to keep your feet at right angles. If you are doing it correctly, "snow" will collect behind the back blade. Learn this stop on each foot.

EDGES

We have been using the word *edge* to mean the inside or outside skating edge of your hollow-ground blade. From now on the word also will be used occasionally to describe the curve traced on the surface of the ice by the edge of your blade. In this chapter and the next, we will describe the four basic edges that can be skated on each foot: *forward outside, forward inside, backward outside,* and *backward inside.* We will describe the technique for skating each of these edges on the right foot—the same principles apply to the left foot.

THE FORWARD OUTSIDE EDGE

While forward outside edges may be a bit more difficult to learn than the forward inside edges you have already begun to work with, we will start with them because it may help you to handle the inside edges without dropping your ankle. Begin gliding on two feet in a curve to the right around an imaginary circle, with your feet close together and your entire body leaning to the right (just as if you were steering a bicycle). Build up some speed and glide in this curve a few times. Your right hip, shoulder,

A two-foot curve to the right.

and arm will lead—with your left shoulder back. You will be looking over your right shoulder in the direction of travel. Your knees are bent, and your body is in a straight line, leaning toward the center of your "circle." The blade nearest the center (the right, in this case) will be on an outside edge, and the left blade will be on an inside edge.

Slowly raise your left foot now and hold it over the tracing you have made in the ice behind you, with the heel just inside the curve. Your left hip should be held back and kept down, actually tucked in below the left shoulder. This is called *keeping the free side down,* and it is very important. In skating the edge, there is a strong tendency for the hips and shoulders to *swing* around in the direction of the curve. Be sure that your body lean is a

A right forward outside edge (RFO).

A right swing roll.

straight line from the top of your head to the edge of your skating blade. When your forward outside edge feels reasonably secure on the right foot, begin on the left: simply translate this description word for word, substituting *right* for *left* and *left* for *right* as you read. This will keep you busy for a while!

CONSECUTIVE FORWARD OUTSIDE EDGES

Consecutive outside edges—that is, alternating right and left forward outside edges—are easier to learn as *swing rolls*. They not only play an important part in more advanced figure and dance moves but also bring a real plus to hockey warm-ups and can be considered one of

the advantages that a figure skater brings to hockey.

As you skate forward on your right outside edge (RFO), begin to draw your free foot forward while your hips, shoulders, and entire body are rotating into neutral position (to squarely face your line of travel). Beginners tend to hold the free foot somewhat to the side; it should always be either directly behind your skating foot, close beside it (so that—ideally—it lightly brushes the other boot as it passes), or directly in front of your skating foot. In a swing roll, your free leg moves forward and is extended and held for a moment in front of your skating foot; then it is brought back alongside the skating foot. As you transfer your weight to the left foot, bend your knees and lean your body to the left. Turn your right foot out (T-

A left forward outside edge (LFO).

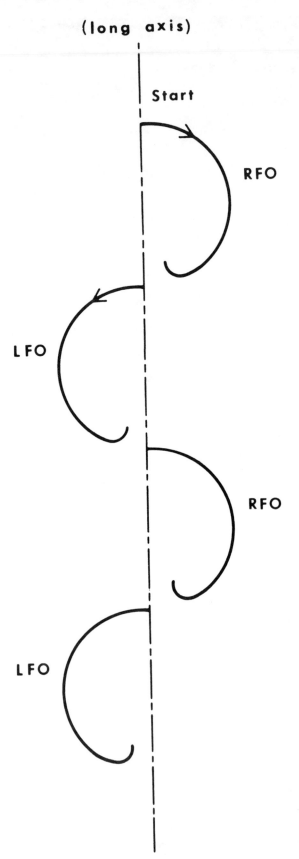

(long axis)

Start

RFO

LFO

RFO

LFO

position) and onto an inside edge. Straighten your right knee, and stroke out onto your left outside edge (LFO).

Whenever possible, you should do these consecutive edges along a *long axis*—an imaginary line along which you can trace (skate) half circles of the same size alternating from side to side. If you look forward to doing *figure eights* eventually, it will help to plan the curves so that the diameter of a full circle would equal about three times your height. In any case, you should complete your roll and return to neutral position by the time you have reached the long axis, where your weight will be transferred to the other foot. On all transfers of weight, the feet are brought parallel and the body assumes neutral position almost simultaneously as the knees begin to bend; then comes the *thrust* (push-off) and the *strike* onto a new skating foot, followed by assumption of your new shoulder and body position.

Diagram of consecutive forward outside edges.

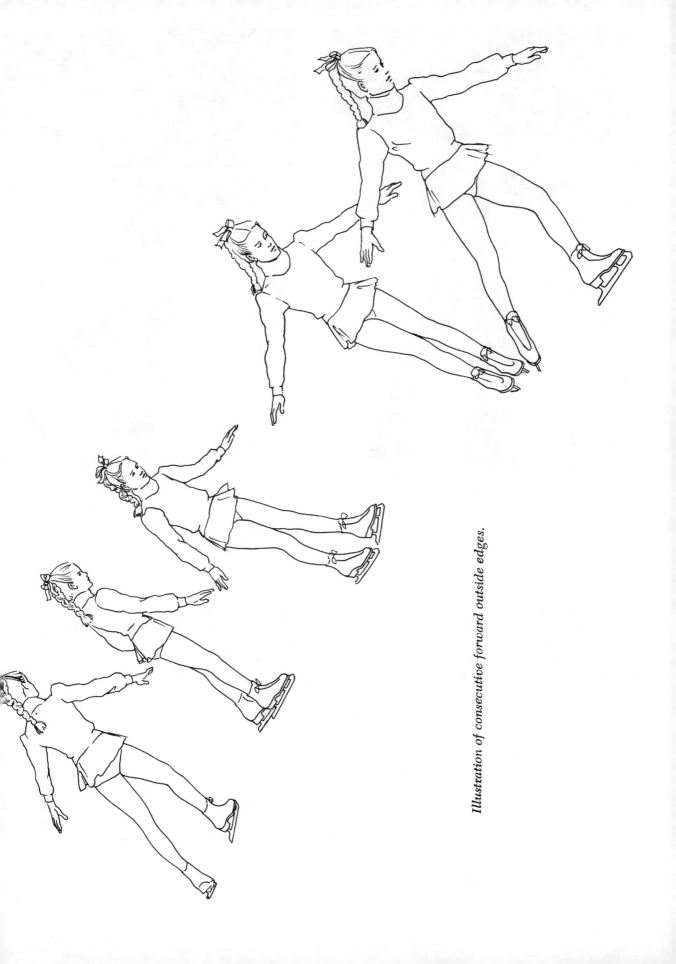

Illustration of consecutive forward outside edges.

A two-foot curve to the left.

A right forward inside edge (RFI).

FORWARD INSIDE EDGES

Most people find the forward inside edges to be easier than the forward outside edges. Since we will describe the forward inside edge on your right foot (RFI), you will begin with both feet on the ice gliding in a curve to your *left*. Again, your body will lean toward the center of the imaginary circle, with the skate nearest the center on an outside edge and the farther (right) skate on an *inside* edge.

This time, however, your shoulders and hips will be square to your line of travel. The left arm can be allowed to move slightly forward and inside the circle, while the right arm remains outside of your curve—the palms of both hands are facing down. Your knees are bent, of course, and only your head is facing toward the center of the circle. At this point, transfer your weight to the right foot entirely, and allow your left leg to move back so that your free foot is held inside the tracing; the heel of your left boot should be directly over the tracing.

Slowly rotating your head, shoulders, and arms to the left, bring your left foot forward. It should pass your skating foot closely if not actually brushing the boot. Stretch your free leg in front of your skating foot and hold it there for a moment, always remembering to keep your free side down so that your hips are level. Now you are ready to transfer your weight to the other foot. Straighten your right knee, and bring your left foot back and parallel to the right. Bend both knees as you establish your body once more in neutral position. Shift your weight, and strike the new edge.

A right forward inside edge with free foot extended.

A crossover to the left: the cross stroke.

Repeat what you did. Begin in neutral position with the arm opposite your skating foot held slightly forward and inside the curve you are tracing. Shoulder and hip positions depend on the size of the circle you are skating. Once you are comfortable and have perfect balance while doing new moves, you can vary the positions somewhat, but *all* stroking calls for the use of neutral position at weight transfer.

FORWARD CROSSOVERS

Crossovers are really a series of *open* strokes (that is, not crossed) each followed by a *cross* stroke: open, cross, open, cross, etc. They are used to round corners or to skate in a circle.

Even more important, you will use them to build up speed as your skating advances. It is essential to learn the technique correctly from the start, for it will serve you well later in any kind of skating and will help you progress more rapidly. Time spent on perfecting your crossovers is time spent wisely.

Probably because most skating is done in a counterclockwise direction, almost everyone can do crossovers more easily this way—and we will describe them only in counterclockwise direction, although you should soon begin to practice them equally in both directions.

It is easier to practice crossovers in a circle at first if you can get the space. Begin your first open stroke on a left forward outside edge, with your right arm and shoulder forward and your right hip pressed down. Your skating knee (in this case, left) should be deeply bent on every stroke, and your lean remains toward the center of the circle. You will develop smoothness only by learning to maintain these positions throughout your crossovers.

During each open stroke, then, your weight will be on your left foot—on an *outside* edge. The cross stroke consists of passing your free foot (in this case, right) around and in front of the toe of your left boot, placing it on an *inside* edge, and transferring your weight. As the right foot takes the weight, bend your right knee (just as deeply as you bent your left knee on the open stroke), straighten your left knee and make a thrust (push off) with the left outside edge. This thrust should be made *outside the curve*, not straight back! As you push off, try holding this position to get the feel of it. An important part of the power you are getting from this series of strokes comes from this thrust from the outside edge.

To continue the cycle, bring your free left foot from its extended position back to parallel your skating foot—keep it straight by a *slight* straightening of your skating leg. Now bend your knees and stroke off again onto the left forward outside edge, this time getting thrust from the inside edge of the right skate as it leaves the ice. Once again, the free leg should be straight and the skating knee bent.

You can practice your crossovers by stepping through them on the floor at home. Remember to hold the same position throughout and to bend the knee taking the ice. As your weight is transferred, the knee of the foot leaving the ice straightens to provide the thrust (from the side of the blade, not the toe). Remember, too, to cross wide over the toe of the skating foot. Don't pick up one foot and place it on the other side of your skating foot as if you were stepping over logs on a campground! The same crossover technique works equally well with hockey or figure skates, and you will find that proper use of it improves your balance and gives a real spurt to your general skating progress.

A crossover to the left: pushing off from the left outside edge.

A crossover to the left: the LFO open stroke.

Executing forward crossovers.

5

Backward Skating—and Some Turns

In backward just as in forward skating, correct posture is of prime importance. Your head is up, back straight, arms and shoulders relaxed, skating knee bent, and free leg in line—as you learned in the last chapter. The most common error in backward skating is the tendency to bend forward from the waist to avoid a backward fall. Probably the second most common error is to alternately stick out one hip and then the other! Both of these habits will hinder your progress in achieving correct balance.

When you are skating backward, your weight should be slightly forward, over the balls of your feet. As you know, the blade of either a figure or hockey skate has a slight curve (the rocker) that allows you to maneuver. For skating backward, your balance point is nearer the front of the blade, and you will find your balance if you think of pressing on the balls of your feet.

THE SIDE-TO-SIDE PUSH

For the beginner, the two methods most often used are the side-to-side push and backward sculling—and they may be combined to advantage. The side-to-side push is easier to adapt to backward stroking although it is harder for some to learn at first.

With your arms and shoulders square, knees bent, weight over both blades, feet fairly close and blades flat (that is, in neutral position), turn both heels to one side (let's say to the right) by twisting *from your waist*. As you do this, your weight will shift to your right foot (the inside edge) while your free left foot rests lightly on the ice beside it. You will feel yourself glide a bit to the right and backward. Bend your knees again and, with another twist from your waist, turn your heels to the left. This time, your weight transfers to your left foot, and you will

A backward glide.

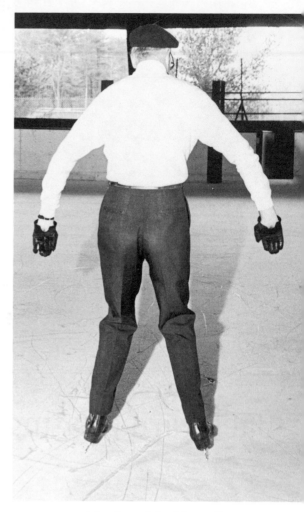

A backward double scull.

move backward to the left. In moving your weight to the side where you point your heels, you create a thrust from the inside edge of the free foot.

You may at first want simply to stand with your heels pointing first one way and then the other, rocking from side to side. Begin to move by pushing away from the foot that is farthest in front of you. Once you gain a little momentum, try to bring your feet together in a straight line and glide as far as possible.

BACKWARD SCULLING

To begin the backward double scull, your toes will be together and your heels apart so that your skate blades are on the inside edges. Think

about your posture. Now bend your knees and let your feet glide apart; when you have reached the width of your shoulders, straighten your knees, come up on the flats of your blades, and draw your feet parallel as you resume neutral position. Repeat this without pausing. Add a backward glide on both feet (close together) as soon as you have some momentum. Alternate this exercise with the side-to-side push to prepare yourself for backward skating.

BACKWARD SINGLE SCULLING

This time you will be drawing capital letter D on the ice with your blades. With your body in neutral position, place most of your weight on the left foot. Your left ankle should be straight.

A backward single scull.

A backward stroke on the right foot.

Turn your right toe in and place that blade on an inside edge. Press down on the right foot, propelling yourself slowly backward. As you do, trace a semi-circle with your right blade and a straight line with your left: a capital D. Now straighten the left knee and pull your feet together. Glide a little way on both feet. Reverse the procedure with the left foot pushing off and tracing a half circle while the right foot traces a straight line. Remember to keep your upper body motionless, and try to travel in a straight line.

BACKWARD STROKING

Backward stroking follows quite naturally once you have mastered the side-to-side push, but it can also begin with single sculling. After you have built up some glide, try it this way: As you push off with your left foot, transfer all your weight to the right foot. Gradually lift the left foot an inch or two from the ice, keeping it in front of you. Press your skating hip forward and down to help maintain your weight over the ball of your skating foot. (Remember, if it is too far forward, your toe pick will catch on the ice; if it is too far back, it is possible to catch your heel in the ice. In either case, you can expect a sudden three-point landing.) Bring your feet back together and—from neutral position—push off with your right inside edge onto your left foot.

Once this feels fairly comfortable, try it from rest. The push-off will be like the one you learned in the side-to-side method. Swing your

A one-foot toe scratch.

A two-foot toe scratch.

left heel out as if to single scull (which puts it on an inside edge); straighten your left knee and push down into the ice, transferring all your weight to the right foot and gliding backward easily on your right outside edge. Work to put this right foot on an outside edge with a good body lean to the right. Practice starting with each foot, and keep your feet close together at each push-off.

BACKWARD STOPPING

There are several ways of stopping backward. If you have figure skates, probably the easiest way

to stop is by using your toe picks. To do a *one-foot toe scratch*, begin gliding slowly backward on both feet. Now slide one blade behind you and raise your heel just enough so that the toe pick scrapes the ice, slows you down, and finally brings you to a stop. Be sure you slide the stopping blade *back*—if you try to do this with your blades parallel, you are likely to lose your balance and fall.

A *two-foot toe scratch* is more difficult to learn, but it has more braking power and it is fun to do. Begin gliding slowly backward again, feet parallel, arms outstretched for balance, body straight. Keeping your body straight, simply lift both heels at once and allow your toe picks to stop you. This requires good balance, since you will lean well forward at the stop, but

44

A backward T-stop.

Neutral position.

you can build your speed up gradually.

There is also a *backward snowplow,* which can be useful to all skaters. As you glide backward on both feet, knees bent, turn one or both toes out—so that the inside edges of your blades shave the ice and bring you to a stop, straightening your knees.

Most difficult is the *backward T-stop.* To do this, you must keep your body square. As you glide backward, place one foot behind you at a right angle; bend your skating knee and lean forward. Stretch the free foot backward and place it lightly on the ice on an inside edge. You will soon learn to adjust the pressure on the stopping blade, since pressing too hard will bring you to a chattering, jarring stop. Do keep your body square throughout.

BACKWARD OUTSIDE EDGES

In forward skating, the inside edges seem to be easier for most skaters; in backward skating, this is reversed, and most skaters find the backward outside edges to be considerably easier. When you are completely comfortable skating backward, it is time to learn the backward or back outside edges.

With your feet together and knees bent in neutral position, sway your body and arms slightly to the left so that you stand momentarily on your left foot. Now push from the inside edge of the left blade, transferring your weight to the right foot as it makes a backward circle on the ice in a counterclockwise direction. Keep that right knee bent, and rotate your

Pushing off onto an RBO edge.

Striking an RBO edge.

shoulders strongly to the right so that your right shoulder and arm are leading. Your skating (right) hip is pressed back hard, and your free (left) foot is held in front of you over the tracing you are making—with the toe pointed down. Your entire body will lean to the right—that is, toward the center of the circle you are tracing on the ice.

As we told you earlier, the push-off is commonly called the *thrust,* and taking the new edge is called the *strike.* Transfer of weight from the thrusting foot (in this case, the left) to the skating foot (right) is gradual. The thrusting foot will actually travel a short distance before the striking foot takes the ice—even at the strike, the weight transfer is just beginning. Both feet remain on the ice for a short distance,

but only just long enough to complete the thrust and weight transfer. You will find that remaining on two feet for too long makes it harder to get on a back outside edge. As you become accustomed to back outside edges, however, you will need less time to complete the thrust and both feet will be on the ice for a very short distance. To thrust onto a left back outside edge (and you should, of course, practice this both ways), simply reverse the above procedure.

CONSECUTIVE BACKWARD OUTSIDE EDGES

To do these as swing rolls, hold the striking position described above until your right back out-

Illustration of consecutive backward outside edges, this time thrusting with the right foot.

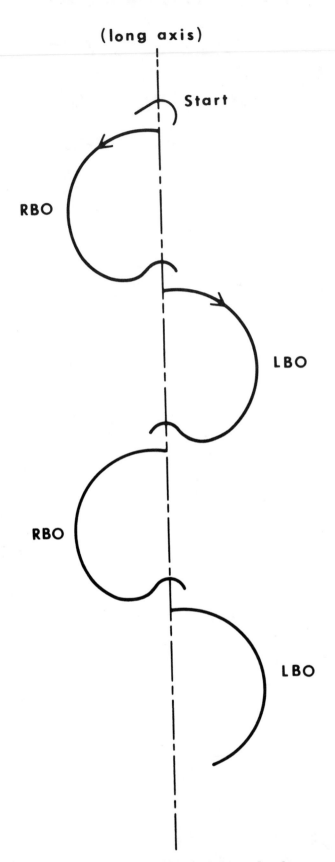

Diagram of consecutive backward outside edges.

LBI edge: preparatory two-foot backward curve to right.

LBI edge: with free foot in back.

side edge is in control. Now slowly allow your free left foot to move back, passing close to the skating foot, until it is extended over your line of travel; while your left foot is moving back, rotate your body slowly until shoulders and hips are once more square. Bring your feet together, bend your knees, and from neutral position strike onto your left back outside edge. This time, of course, the push-off is from the inside edge of the right blade. It may be a little harder when you are already in motion, but the principle is the same. Always be sure to turn the heel of your thrusting foot out all the way, and make your strike with your feet as close together as possible. As with forward swing rolls, a future figure skater would be wise to do these from the first along a long axis.

BACKWARD INSIDE EDGES

Backward inside edges follow quite naturally from backward stroking. A good way to begin these is by skating backward in a slight clockwise curve. Pick up the right skate and extend it in back just inside the tracing. Your right shoulder and hip should be pressed back, and you are looking back over your right shoulder. Your left knee is bent, body lean is to the right, and your free foot is extended in back. When you lose speed, bring your feet together, and from neutral position try this on your right foot.

To do backward inside edges from rest, stand with your back to the long axis, feet about shoulder width apart. Rock onto your left foot; bring the right foot next to it, and make a semi-

LBI edge: close-up of hip position with free foot in back.

RBI edge: starting position.

circular thrust with the left foot, turning your body so that the arms swing to the left. Your right knee is bent, and your left arm remains slightly forward during the strike. Body lean, of course, is to the left (toward the center of the circle) as your right foot strikes the inside back edge. Your left shoulder should be pressed forward and your left foot should be in front as you glide backward. Practice this on each foot— it takes time!

Because they are a problem for most people, the consecutive back inside edges are seldom done as swing rolls. We will describe them briefly as simple back inside edges. Once you have control of your strike, begin to draw your free (left) foot back slowly until it is alongside

the skating foot. With your weight still on the right foot as you approach the long axis, move the left foot slightly behind the skating foot and turn the heel out—allowing your whole body to rotate with it. Now bend your knees and place your left foot on the ice squarely across the long axis. Your right foot makes the thrust that pushes you off onto a back left inside edge. Weight is transferred gradually, and your right foot leaves the ice directly in front of your new skating foot. Your right arm and shoulder remain pressed forward as you glide backward on your left inside edge. Whether or not you intend to continue into advanced figure skating, working with the long axis makes it easier to learn the correct angle for your new strike.

RBI edge: the push-off.

RBI edge: position of free shoulder and foot.

RBI edge: drawing the free foot back.

Backward crossovers to the right.

BACKWARD CROSSOVERS

Once you have learned to skate backward with good balance and some speed, you are likely to find these easier to learn and far less awkward than forward crossovers. They are also easier to do in both directions. Backward crossovers are used to go around corners, skate in circles, and to generate speed in backward skating. Like forward crossovers, they can be practiced on the floor before you try them on the ice.

To do backward crossovers in a counterclockwise direction, you will cross the left foot in front of the right foot—transferring your weight from your right back outside edge to your left

back inside edge. Begin by moving backward on both feet in a counterclockwise direction with your right shoulder and arm back in a strongly *checked* position (this means simply a position held firmly with no motion allowed—it will prevent rotation and keep you on the curve you have started on). Your head will face the center of the circle you are making. Both knees are bent, and your right hip is pressed forward to keep your weight over your skating foot. Your entire body leans to the right to make sure that you are well on the right outside edge. (Beginners often resist this edge, resulting in the right foot making a spiral tracing as it flops from outside to inside.)

Now make a sculling thrust with your left

foot, but leave it on the ice. Still on the ice but not bearing weight, move the left foot across in front of the skating foot, crossing the legs at the ankles and lifting your right foot off the ice as you transfer your weight to the back inside edge of your left blade. Don't let the toe picks scratch the ice, and be sure your right knee is bent at all times. As you become a better skater, you will be able to use the outside edge of your right foot to provide additional thrust and more power in your backward crossovers.

The crossover may be repeated by bringing the right foot out of its crossed position and placing it next to the left foot as you continue skating backward in a counterclockwise direction. Even faster and more powerful stroking can be achieved by placing the right foot inside the circle and in a *leading* position. This is quite a departure from most skating, where the feet are always brought together before the new movement. It allows the skater to sweep over a larger portion of ice while remaining over his center of gravity—and thus to "pull" for more speed. The deeper the knee bend, the more speed will result. Done correctly, the left foot never leaves the ice.

Backward crossovers should also be learned in a clockwise direction, which many skaters find easier. In this case, the right foot crosses in front of the left; the left arm and shoulder are back, and you face left toward the center of the circle you are tracing.

Forward-to-back turn, first sliding one foot ahead.

After the forward-to-back turn.

TURNS FROM FORWARD TO BACKWARD

Somewhere along the line as you are mastering backward skating, you will want a simple way to turn from forward to back and also from backward to forward. We will instruct you first in the turns we consider to be the easiest.

The simplest method of turning backward is to glide (slowly at first) on two feet and then abruptly twist the upper body (head, shoulders, and arms) and hips to the right or to the left, turning the lower body to join it. This should result in a two-foot backward glide. You can also turn by sliding one foot ahead of the other and then sliding it around so that it heads backward. The other foot (and the rest of your body) will

want to join it, and you can then bring your feet together for the glide backward.

FROM BACKWARD TO FORWARD

Admittedly, turns from backward to forward are awkward for most beginners. Advanced skaters most often use a crossover before turning forward, but you should leave that for later. The turn we will describe here begins with the skater's back toward the curve he or she is making. If this is a turn from a right back outside edge to a left forward outside edge, the left side should be leading, the right side pressed back. By bringing the free foot up to approximately the instep of the skating foot, it should be easy

Back-to-forward turn: free foot at instep.   *Back-to-forward turn: stroking onto LFO edge.*

to strike off onto a forward outside edge. To prevent your free side from swinging around, handle this as you would a push-off for consecutive outside edges: have the left side leading, with the right (free) side pressed down—especially the hip and leg, which should be held in line in back over the tracing.

As this becomes comfortable, work to bring the free foot up to the heel of the skating foot before turning forward. Try to skate the new curve on nearly the same arc as the first, rather than going off in a new direction. This turn requires strongly checked positions.

6

Hockey Skating

If you want to play hockey, the first thing you will need is to know the basic principles of skating: forward skating, backward skating, the crossovers (sometimes called *cuts* in hockey) in both directions as well as forward and back, plus some stops and turns. Check your skating skills against those described in Chapters 4 and 5. It will save you time and give you a real advantage in learning the game.

Obviously, the next thing you will need is proper equipment—beginning with a good pair of hockey skates, a stick, and a puck. Don't hesitate to ask the best hockey players you know for advice. Again, get the best pair of skates you can afford, and make sure they fit properly. Also, since hockey is a contact sport, some pre-

cautions are needed to avoid injury. Even if you are just playing shinny on a local pond, a heavy sweater, sturdy blue jeans, and hockey gloves or heavy mittens should be worn. The puck should be kept *on the ice*—no "lifties" allowed. The most common injuries in hockey are cuts on the face during play from the stick or from the skate of another player during a fall. Head injuries can be very serious and have caused some deaths. For an organized game, proper equipment is essential. Players or their parents must be willing to spend some $200 or more for a good stick, shin guards, protective pants, helmet, gloves, and face mask. These all help minimize injuries and give the hockey player confidence to perform at his or her best.

1980 Olympic hockey, U.S. versus U.S.S.R.: fourth goal for the United States. (Wide World Photos)

1980 Olympic hockey, U.S. versus U.S.S.R.: a save by U.S. goalie James Craig. (Wide World Photos)

Skating posture for hockey.

Pushing off (note entire left blade is on ice, knees are flexed).

HOCKEY STYLE

For hockey, your skating posture will be entirely different from recreational or figure skating. Your body will be bent *forward* from the waist much of the time, knees deeply bent, and feet about shoulder width apart. Your thrust is made by pushing from the hip, and—as you learned before—the entire blade must be on the ice so that you can thrust from the center of the blade. This is particularly important in hockey because pushing from the toe or heel will cause a loss of power. *The whole idea of hockey skating style is to conserve and direct power when and where it is needed.* Your head and shoulders should be relaxed. The forward lean keeps your upper body slightly ahead of your hips and helps make possible powerful forward strokes. This lean also

helps you to take collisions with other players; if you skate in an upright position, you will soon find yourself being continually knocked off your feet.

Flexible knee action is very important. The only time the knee should be straightened is at the end of a thrust, just before the skate comes off the ice to move forward for another stroke. A hockey skater's knee should always be ahead of the skating foot—this keeps the skate blade under the body for proper balance and permits a quick change of direction. You must also avoid raising the skate too high off the ice when stroking, since this also wastes power and interferes with your speed and proper balance.

In skating backward, you will still lean forward from the waist with knees bent to keep your body weight directly over the blades. Powerful backward stroking in hockey comes from pushing off with the inside edges of the right and left blades while alternately swinging the hips to left and right. It is particularly important in skating backward to keep your hips low by deeply bending your knees so you won't find yourself skating on the tips of your blades.

PREPARATION FOR HOCKEY

Colleges, prep schools, and even high schools today demand a certain level of skating ability before accepting an individual on the hockey squad. One way to learn these skills is through organized hockey (such as peewees and local hockey clinics), but you can do a lot to help yourself. Hockey requires two skills primarily: skating and stick-handling. A good hockey player must be a good skater, but he must also be able to put the puck in the net. The best way to learn stick-handling is from actual play, but there are many things you can learn from watching a game or from skating around on a Saturday or Sunday afternoon.

The most important thing is always to skate with a hockey stick (better yet, with a stick and a puck) if your ice rink allows it. This will teach you balance and help you learn stick control. When you skate with a puck, learn to skate without watching the puck all the time. When you watch good hockey players, you will see that they control the puck merely by the feel of it on the stick and only look at it when they maneuver or pass to another player. You should also learn to "carry" the puck while skating backward—this is often necessary to avoid opposing players. You can also practice maneuvering the puck around the ice with your feet. This is important because players often have to "dig" the puck off the boards with their skate blades—particularly in crowded situations where sticks can't be brought into play. Skate around the rink a few times just kicking the puck with your feet, and practice kicking it into and off the boards.

Fast starts (called *breakaways*) and stops are extremely important in hockey; in fact, there is a saying that "the shortest distance between two points is a start and a stop." If you take a curved path, you will have to travel farther, and it will take you longer.

A hockey stop to the left . . .

SUDDEN STOPS

For the hockey player, sudden stops are a serious matter. The quickest way to stop on ice is the well-known *hockey stop*, which we described briefly in Chapter 4. The hockey player swings his entire body (shoulders, hips, and both feet) abruptly around in a right angle to right or left, at the same time sharply bending his knees, throwing his weight backward, and digging his blades into the ice. When you turn to the right, you will use the outside edge of the right skate and the inside edge of the left skate —and most of the strain will be taken by your right leg. When you turn to the left, this is simply reversed. Practice hockey stops in both di-

. . . and a hockey stop to the right.

Practicing a stopping exercise.

rections, making sure you come to a complete *stop* and not just coasting around in a circle!

The hockey stop can be modified by taking all the load on the inside foot (outside edge) and raising the other foot slightly off the ice. This allows a faster change of direction but requires very strong ankle and leg muscles since the inside leg carries all the load.

Backward stops are done in two ways. In the *stem stop,* a form of the snowplow, both skates are turned with toes facing outward; knees are brought together; the body leans forward, and both legs are straightened as the inside edges of the skates are pushed into the ice. In the *side stop,* both body and skates are turned quickly to either right or left; knees are bent; and legs are gradually straightened as the skates are pressed

sideways into the ice. It is also possible to do a one-legged side stop by turning one skate sideways and pushing it hard into the ice as you lean forward.

It is impossible to overemphasize the importance of fast stops in hockey. There is a stopping exercise beginners can practice alone in a corner of the rink. Stand with your feet about shoulder width apart, leaning forward and with knees bent. Take a stroke directly to the side with your right foot; turn your body and your right skate to the left and stop, using the inside edge of the right skate, without putting your left foot on the ice. Now take a stroke directly to the side with your left foot and repeat, this time turning to the right. Do this twenty or thirty times each time you are at the ice rink.

FAST BREAKAWAYS

For a fast breakaway, you will take from four to six short, choppy, rapid strokes to get moving; knees are strongly bent, the body leans forward, and the inside edges dig hard into the ice on each thrust. Once you are underway, of course, the strokes are lengthened and you will push strongly from the hips. You must be able to make a quick breakaway in any direction at any time—forward, back, to right, or to left—and from any position.

Practice your breakaways. Starting from rest, skate as hard as you can forward for twenty or thirty feet and do a hockey stop turning to the right. Repeat, doing a hockey stop to the left. The fast breakaway should be done in different directions, such as directly to your left for twenty or thirty feet, followed by a hockey stop. You should also practice by turning 180 degrees (from front to back) and skating hard to the rear as if you were a defenseman trying to get back to cover the net (this is known as a *turn-and-go drill*). Be sure to alternate your turns, to the right one time, to the left the next.

A slightly different version is the quick breakaway from coasting. While skating around the rink, bring your feet close together and coast (glide) for thirty feet or so. Then suddenly make a quick breakaway, skating forward as fast as possible for perhaps another thirty feet. You can repeat this several times around the rink.

A hockey crossover to the left . . .

FAST BACKWARD SKATING

Being able to skate backward rapidly is particularly important if you want to play defense, since it is essential to quickly pick up opposing players who start to bring the puck down the ice. Even a forward should skate backward quickly and easily, however, since you never know when it will be necessary to play defense —such as a sudden rush by opponents or perhaps when "killing penalties."

Starting from rest, practice the quick break backward by bending your knees and pushing as hard as you can to develop fast backward stroking. Alternately push with the inside edges of your blades, adding power with a strong fast swing of the hips.

CROSSOVERS (CUTS)

Have you ever seen a kid showing off fast crossovers to the left at a public skating session—yet when you ask to see crossovers to the right, he or she is lost? A very common warm-up drill for hockey players is to do crossovers in a large figure-eight pattern, going to the right at one end of the rink and to the left at the other end. It is important that you are actually doing crossovers, not just coasting around the circles. Even during a public skating session, you may be able to go to the center of the ice to practice crossovers to your right (clockwise). Some rinks periodically reverse the direction of skating to give everyone a chance to skate in a clockwise direction—you might ask your rink manager about this if it is not being done at your favorite rink.

. . . and a hockey crossover to the right.

It is also a good idea to learn backward crossovers in both directions, and these can be practiced by going around a figure-eight pattern as in the case of forward crossovers. Even though these are not terribly important to your game, they are good to have in your "bag of tricks."

SWING-AROUNDS

The hockey *swing-around* is a very important way to change direction quickly by making a small half circle on the ice. In the two-legged swing-around, you lean forward, bend the knees, and then lean sharply into the inside of the circle while keeping both skates on the ice. This can be done in either direction, and it should be practiced regularly both ways. It is by far the

fastest way to turn around, much faster than a hockey stop followed by a fast break in a new direction.

It is also possible to do a one-legged swing-around, taking all the weight on the inner leg and lifting the outer leg off the ice as you make the turn. This is even faster than the two-legged version, since the free leg is immediately available to begin stroking to the rear. It is much more difficult to learn, however, and probably best left to the advanced skater.

POWER SKATING

You may hear a lot of talk about *power skating.* This term was proposed several years ago to describe a training program designed primarily to develop speed on the ice. All it really means is learning proper skating technique, and it is something you can work on whenever you are on the ice. As you start off skating slowly around the rink to warm up, lean forward with knees well bent and push with the inside edges of your blades. Gradually increase your speed with stronger stroking. Concentrate on developing a smooth, relaxed, and effortless stroke with flexible knees and good balance. Many young skaters try to build up endurance with fast laps around the rink, but this serves no useful purpose when they are merely reinforcing bad skating habits they may have learned. Your main effort should be directed toward proper technique. Agility and technique are far more important than mere power in the game of hockey.

GETTING IN SHAPE—AND STAYING THAT WAY

Most coaches feel that the best way to warm up is by actually skating on the ice. This should involve a general "loosening" of the joints, so that the muscles you will use later are ready. Hockey players are particularly susceptible to muscle pulls and groin strains because of the continual fast and abrupt stops and starts; proper conditioning and warm-up are extremely important to help avoid these injuries. Even when there is insufficient time for proper warming up on the ice, special exercises can be done in the dressing room before your skates are put on. Bending, stretching, and running in place can be used as a substitute for on-ice exercises. It is also a very good idea to do some loosening-up exercises whenever you have to sit out for a time, such as between periods of a game.

What can a hockey skater do during those periods of the year when there is no ice for skating? Since you must remain in good physical condition, almost any kind of exercise will help. Running and bicycling will improve your wind and endurance. Bending exercises will strengthen the muscles you use for stops and starts. Some players practice squeezing special spring-loaded "gadgets" to strengthen their fingers and wrists. Goal-tenders find that playing handball helps to sharpen their eyes and their reactions. However, the unfortunate truth is that most skating skills involve the use of muscles different from those used in other sports. Off-ice exercises can help in your general conditioning but are no real substitute for skating itself. If you are serious about playing hockey, you will be on the ice every chance you get.

7

Speed Skating

•

Although speed skating had become popular throughout England by the 1870s, there was complete lack of regulation of the sport. Amateurs competed against professionals, and some races involved very handsome cash prizes. Betting and sweepstakes were commonplace. When the National Skating Association of Great Britain was founded in 1879, one of the decisions made at its first meeting was to promote the establishment of speed skating contests under the direction of an international skating council. The International Skating Union was established in 1892 at a meeting in Scheveningen, Netherlands, as a world body to organize and regulate skating—and its primary concern was for speed skating.

The first international amateur speed skating contest was held at Amsterdam during the winter of 1892–93. Competition consisted of four distances: 500, 1,500, 5,000, and 10,000 meters. To be crowned Champion of the World, a skater was required to win three of the four races, and Jaap Edan of the Netherlands became the first ISU champion when he won the first three races that year.

Speed skating became an Olympic event in 1924 for men and in 1960 for women. Olympic-style racing differs from the usual rough-and-tumble "pack" races, in which a group of competitors bursts from the starting gate (and the winner is often the skater who is best at jockeying or pushing others out of the way). To avoid this, Olympic racing involves only two skaters on the 400-meter track at one time. In effect, they are racing against the clock rather than each other, and the winner is simply the skater who has the fastest time in any particular race. Men skate 500- and 1,000-meter sprints and

This start of a skating race in Canada about 1900 illustrates "pack" racing. (By permission of Notman Photographic Archives, McCord Museum, McGill University, Montreal)

1,500-, 5,000-, and 10,000-meter races; women skate 500- and 1,000-meter sprints and 1,500- and 3,000-meter races.

SPEED SKATING TECHNIQUE

It is not wise to try to learn to skate first on speed skates. The long flat blades are hard to handle, and—because they are potentially more dangerous than hockey or figure skates—many ice rinks do not permit them to be used at all. The time to buy your first pair of speed skates is after you have learned to handle yourself easily on hockey or figure skates and are quite sure that you are most interested in speed skating.

Speed skating is entirely different from the other types of skating. It involves powerful forward stroking and fast counterclockwise turning to the left; outside edges, backward skating, sudden stops, and "fancy" skating movements are not part of the speed skating picture. It is probably no exaggeration to say that about 85 per cent of the body positions you will use in speed skating are unnatural, and it is important to begin at a fairly young age since the beginner will instinctively tend to do the wrong thing.

The first thing you will have to do is get used to your skates, very probably at the cost of a few spills on the ice. At this point it will help to take lessons or to join a speed skating club where you can learn some of the basic techniques. If this is not possible at first, try to watch some good speed skaters and imitate them. Learn to skate in a crouched position with arms in back, holding the left wrist with the right hand or vice versa. Try to develop the powerful energy-saving glide of the speed skater, always being sure you push with the entire blade. Practice your counterclockwise cross-

Eric Heiden, of Madison, Wisconsin, winning his fourth Olympic gold medal at Lake Placid on February 21, 1980. (Wide World Photos)

overs, using a strong inward lean and pushing directly to the outside of the circle with both blades. Your primary concern should be on control and good body position; the speed will come later.

COMPETITION

When you begin to feel really comfortable on speed skates, you will probably want to start racing. Sooner or later some type of professional instruction is essential if you have any intention of becoming a serious competitor. Three factors determine your success in competition: power, conditioning, and technique.

Since most speed skating is simply a matter of more or less brute force applied to the ice, the powerful skater will obviously have an advantage. Eric Heiden is an excellent example: over

six feet tall and with twenty-nine-inch thighs, he literally *powers* his way down the ice. After competing in the 1976 Olympics at the age of seventeen, he became in the following year the first United Skates skater since 1891 to win the men's All-Around World Speed Skating Championship. At the 1980 Olympics in Lake Placid, Eric made a clean sweep of speed-skating competition, winning the 500-, 1,000-, 1,500-, 5,000-, and 10,000-meter events.

A second important factor is conditioning. A serious speed skater recognizes that training is an all-year-round proposition. During the winter season, competitive skaters usually practice twice daily, doing laps at various speeds to develop both technique and endurance. To build up strength, they also lift weights, run sprints, climb hills, and do exercises specifically designed for speed skaters. During the off-season, they use "land-skating" techniques, such

Gaetan Boucher of Canada. (Wide World Photos)

as climbing hills sideways, "low-walking" to practice the crouched position, and simulated stroking. Many of them use special skates with rollers in place of blades. A special skateboard has been designed to permit a speed skater to practice stroking, particularly thrust and recuperation. The United States Olympic Committee invites top speed skaters to a special high-altitude, two-week summer training program in Colorado Springs to further develop strength and endurance.

The third factor, technique, is one area where the Europeans (particularly the Soviets) are way ahead of the United States. The position of the body, the inclination of head and shoulders, proper stroking, the swing of the arms, and the correct use of centrifugal force on the turns—details such as these greatly affect the speed of the skater. Proper co-ordination of arm and leg movements is critical. Even slight bobbing up and down is a clear indication that energy is being wasted. Also, because wind resistance must be reduced to a minimum, speed skating "uniforms" are now made of very smooth, skin-tight nylon. Where races can be won or lost by hundredths of a second, the proper clothing can save *tenths* of a second.

A dramatic example of the importance of technique was demonstrated by Gaetan Boucher of Canada at Davos, Switzerland, in January of 1981. Only 5 feet 8 inches tall and weighing 151 pounds, Boucher was able to break Eric Heiden's world record in the 1,000-meter sprint. In speed skating, the tall man does not necessarily win over the short man!

OLYMPIC-STYLE SPEED SKATING TECHNIQUE

Speed skating movements can be divided into four categories: (1) the start; (2) the straightaway sprint; (3) the straightaway glide, used in the longer races; and (4) the turns. Each involves a separate technique.

In Olympic skating, when the starter says, "To your mark!" the two skaters assume starting position through the "Ready!" command. They break down the track at the instant the starter fires the gun that triggers the electronic timing system. Any movement before the gun goes off

is considered a false start; three false starts result in disqualification. The time of the race is recorded electronically when a skater breaks a beam of light at the finish line. Races are timed to hundredths of a second.

At the start of a race, the skater stands ready, leaning forward and facing down the track with knees bent, skates parallel about shoulder width apart and at an angle of 40 to 45 degrees to the starting line. Skates are slightly on an inside edge, body weight is evenly distributed over the blades, knees are together, the right arm is back at shoulder height, and the left hand is in front of the left knee. With the starting gun, the skater makes a powerful thrust with the right foot, leaning forward and quickly straightening the body and right leg. The right arm swings rapidly forward in front of the chest to give impetus to the stroke; the left arm, held straight, is swung diagonally backward and to the side. Like a coiled spring, the body lunges directly down the track. The left skate is turned outward in preparation for the next stroke.

The first stroke with the left foot is short, usually without a glide. The blade is placed on the ice with the heel slightly beyond the starting line. The left arm swings diagonally forward in front of the body, and the right arm swings diagonally backward and to the side. The first three to five "running steps" are short, and the arm swings are also short. With each stroke, the glide is lengthened and the body position is lowered gradually by leaning forward and increasing the bend of the legs. By the end of the seventh step, the skater should be in usual skating stride; any additional running only keeps the skater from building up more speed and uses up too much energy for the distance covered.

In the longer races (3,000-, 5,000-, and 10,000 meters), arms are clasped behind the back for the entire distance after the start. This best conserves energy and permits use of the power glide. On the turns, the skater leans to the left and pushes directly to the side with the blade—keeping shoulders and hips parallel to the ice. It is very important not to raise the body on turns, since this makes pushing directly to the side more difficult and thereby causes loss of power. Arms are not swung on the turns during longer races unless the skater is trying to make up time.

In the 500-meter sprint, however, the arms swing continuously. In the straightaway, the arms swing downward and diagonally backward with palms up and thumbs toward the body. Ideally, the backward swing should be no higher than the shoulder—anything higher wastes energy. On the forward swing, the elbow is bent so that the hand is approximately in front of the opposite shoulder. In 1,000- and 1,500-meter races, swinging of both arms uses too much energy, and normally only the right arm is swung. On the turns, however, both arms may be swung, and often these races end with both arms swinging madly.

It is often said that more races have been won or lost in the turns than in any other part of the track. Centrifugal force can be a friend or a foe, depending on how it is used. The laws of physics tell us that, if a body moves in a circle at constant speed, a force must be exerted perpendicular to the direction of motion and directed toward the center (of the circle the skater is traversing). This requires a strong lean to the left, with the push of the blades directly outward. Several transition steps are taken in preparing for a turn, and there is a similar transition period in coming out of a turn. Good skaters actually gain speed in the turns, pouring on power with the last few strokes as they make the transition back to the straightaway.

Proper use of arm swing is particularly important on the turns. The right arm swings hard forward; as it passes the body, the right thumb is kept down and the palm out to keep the right shoulder forward. The left arm is swung hard back with palm up. The forward swing of the left arm has little value and may cause problems if swung too far; for this reason, the forward swing of the left arm is easy, with the elbow sharply bent so that the hand is roughly in front of the left collarbone. Shoulders remain parallel to the ice at all times, and it is important not to lower or advance the left shoulder.

It is essential to maintain the crouched position throughout with no bobbing or weaving, smooth easy stroking, and a smooth transition between turns and straightaways. Shoulders and upper trunk are held rigid with shoulders parallel to the ice except in the longer races, where they roll very slightly. Hips are always parallel to the ice and at right angles to the track of the skater.

Unfortunately, there are no books that cover the essentials of speed skating. The final chapter of this book lists several organizations that promote and encourage speed skating, and they have some booklets that may be helpful to you. These organizations also sponsor competitions and will arrange for suitable coaching of promising young speed skaters. Since only a small number of ice rinks are available to speed skaters, the sport is at present very much limited to the East and Midwest. As a result, speed skating is not one of the more popular sports in the United States—and, in view of this, it is interesting to note that our speed skaters have always done remarkably well in Olympic competition.

8

Figure Skating

Figure skating can be divided into four general categories: (1) the compulsory figures, (2) free skating, (3) pair skating, and (4) ice dancing. Rules for each of these are established by the International Skating Union (ISU). In the United States, the governing body for figure skating is the United States Figure Skating Association (USFSA), which conducts tests, maintains records, sponsors competitions and exhibitions, and publishes *Skating* magazine. The USFSA has several hundred member clubs scattered throughout the United States, and—if you are going to pursue figure skating seriously—you certainly should become a member of USFSA and your local skating club.

THE COMPULSORY FIGURES

One of the first things you will want to do is to buy a copy of the USFSA *Rulebook* and learn about the unique series of tracings that have given figure skating its name. They are called *figures* because at one time skaters actually tried to trace numerals onto the ice surface. Some of the old-time skaters had such control of their bodies that they were able to make intricate patterns and designs such as Maltese crosses and grapevines and even develop their own original figures; in fact, for many years part of every figure skating competition involved skating an original figure!

In times past, these tracings were known as the *school figures,* but in today's competition they are called the *compulsory figures.* The patterns to be skated in each competition are selected by drawing lots, and all competitors must then skate the same figures. While figures have accounted in the past for as much as 60 per cent of a skater's total score, they are now worth only 30 per cent in advanced events. *Free skating* (which consists of jumps, spins, and other movements incorporated into a program set to music of the skater's choice) is far better known to the public and has gradually received more emphasis and an ever-increasing percentage of the competing skater's final score.

Many people have never seen the compulsory figures skated. This is not too surprising, since they are seldom practiced at general skating sessions and are rarely televised at competitions. They must be skated on a clean sheet of ice ("new ice"), so that the tracings can be seen clearly by the skaters themselves and so that they can be judged in a test or in competition without being obscured by other marks on the ice. After each skater has traced a figure, the judges examine the print. Sometimes they sweep the tracing with a small brush to remove any "snow," and they quite often get down on their hands and knees to examine the figure.

In a practice session at the local ice rink, a figure skater usually rents a *patch* of ice—that is, a strip of clean ice about twenty feet wide and half the width of the rink. Patch sessions are often run by the skating clubs, some of them in the early hours of the morning so that serious young skaters may practice their figures each day before they go off to school. Patch sessions (and free skating sessions) are usually scheduled before and after school hours although this varies on weekends and during vacations. In addition, many clubs provide special "summer schools," where skaters may practice all day long for several weeks.

If you enter a rink during a patch session, you will notice at once how quiet it is. A great deal of concentration is necessary in skating figures, and sometimes the only sound is the whispering of blades on the ice and an occasional crunching of the ice from a push-off. In recent years some clubs have begun to play music during patch sessions, but most skaters still prefer the quiet.

Figures are based on circles. In today's com-petition, they consist of either two or three circles that are skated without stopping and, if possible, with a constant speed. Each figure must be skated three times on each foot. The idea is to skate the figure as accurately as possible, as though it were drawn by a compass, and then to repeat it two more times (this is called *superimposition*). Since the human body is not perfect, the figures traced are never entirely perfect either, and they are judged by the degree of error as well as by the form and style of the skater.

During practice sessions, the skater may use a collapsible metal compass called a *scribe* to measure circles. The scribe has a point that is used to draw perfect circles over the ones the skater has made on the ice—so that errors can easily be seen. Some skaters draw circles with a scribe first and then try to skate on these pre-drawn circles, but this is discouraged by many coaches; the scribe may become a crutch and can actually inhibit the natural motion of the skater, which is necessary for good circles. In tests and competitions, the use of scribes is prohibited even during warm-up.

As your figure skating improves, you will probably want to become involved in the testing program. At lower levels, skating clubs often have badge and ribbon programs consisting of instruction in groups and a series of tests. The USFSA begins with a basic skills test, and the Ice Skating Institute of America (ISIA) has other tests from very basic to quite high levels and difficult requirements. The Canadian Figure Skating Association (CFSA) has its own test structure, and this is the case in most countries where figure skating is organized. Besides its National Skating Test Schedule, CFSA also conducts a Power Skating program. In all countries, tests are judged by people who have been trained specifically to be judges by their figure skating associations.

The regular testing program of the USFSA includes a fairly easy Preliminary Test and eight Figure Tests. In general, these become increasingly difficult as you move up—with the differences between test levels becoming steeper. If you should decide to enter competition, you will find that your test level determines the category in which you may compete. Many local competitions include categories for skaters at each level. Before you may compete in the senior events that make you eligible for world or Olympic competition, you will be required to pass all eight Figure Tests plus the Senior Free Skating Test. While it has happened that a skater has been able to pass the eighth test as early as age nine, this is very unusual. It is a long climb, and of the many who begin the USFSA test structure, very few make it to the top.

In the meanwhile, before you begin serious work on the compulsory figures, you would be wise to master the following three basic figure skating movements: the *three turns*, the *mohawks*, and *changes of edge*.

THREE TURNS

These turns are used in certain of the compulsory figures as well as in free skating and ice dancing. They are all turns on one foot from an outside to an inside edge or from an inside to an outside edge, and they may begin from forward or backward skating. In each case, the rotation is in the same direction as the natural curve of the edge you are skating. The *right forward outside three,* which we will describe for you, is begun on an RFO edge (a *clockwise* edge), and your turn will be in a clockwise direction. As you may have guessed, the resulting mark or tracing on the ice will resemble the numeral "3."

The three turns are all named for the edge you begin on. As you skate on an RFO edge, then, rotate your shoulders until the left arm and shoulder are in front with the free left leg behind and the foot pointing down over your tracing. Continue to rotate your head, shoulders, and hips sharply to the right, at the same time bringing your free foot up behind your right foot. As you do this, straighten your skating knee. *The twisting of your upper body combined with the release of weight over the blade from raising your right knee will cause the skate to turn around!* This is actually the easiest part of your turn, but we will return to it with some refinements shortly.

Let's see now what happens when the skate turns around. This is the point where the beginner often loses control. As soon as your foot turns, your free (left) arm, shoulder, and hip must be pressed back—this time with the free foot pointing down and over the tracing in front

RFO three turn: the preparatory rotation.

RFO three turn: bringing the free foot up behind.

RFO three turn: after the turn to RBI—the check.

of you. Your head always faces in the direction you are traveling. These are the details that *check* your turn—that is, they stop your rotation to the right and make it possible for you to hold your new back inside edge.

Now for some of the fine points: As you prepare for the three turn, be sure your shoulders and hips are turning in toward your edge (RFO in this case, so that you are turning them to the right). Your weight is just back of the center of your blade as usual, and your posture is erect. The free foot should point down both before and after the turn. Try to get the feeling of *rolling* in and out of the turn. While you must move very gradually into your rotation, when you reach the point where you are prepared to turn, turn quickly and check quickly. Be sure no part of your body "anticipates" the turn—if any part slips into checked position before your skating foot turns, your three will never look quite smooth (this is known as *pulling the three*). It is also important to press the free hip down both before and after the turn and to keep the free leg close in as the turn is being made.

Three turns used in ice dancing include the *waltz three*, the *dropped three,* and the *quick drop three,* but you will not have to worry about these for some time.

MOHAWKS

The term *mohawk* comes from what was once thought to be a similar move done in a war dance of the Mohawk Indians. Mohawks are used in free skating and in ice dancing; although not used in the compulsory figures, they are good preparation for some of the movements that are used in the figures. They are turns from a forward edge to a backward edge of the same type (that is, left forward inside to right back inside edge, right forward inside to left back inside, and so on) changing from one foot to another.* The most common (and easiest) is the *forward inside open mohawk*. While it can and should be done in both directions, we will describe the one that begins on a right forward inside edge.

You will start this mohawk on an RFI edge, in neutral position with bent skating knee. When the edge feels secure, begin to rotate to your left (counterclockwise), so that your right shoulder leads. Continue rotating your body until both shoulders and head face the tracing, and bring the heel of your free left foot next to the instep of your skating foot at a right angle (this will remind you of T-position). Now place your left foot on the ice on an inside edge with weight on the ball of your foot, gently but firmly press back the right side of your body (the new free side) to check your turn, and extend your right foot over your tracing. The back edge for the mohawk is essentially the same as for the three turn, with a strong check required in both cases.

What we have described is called an *open* mohawk because the new free foot goes back after the turn. (Closed inside mohawks are used only in advanced dances and can be learned later.) What makes this mohawk work, of course, is the strong rotation of your body before the turn. If you fail to rotate far enough, you are likely to get a snowy, scraped turn—that is, your left foot will come down on an out-

* There are similar turns from backward to forward, but the name mohawk is seldom applied to them.

RFI to LBI open mohawk: the RFI edge.

RFI to LBI open mohawk: preparatory rotation.

RFI to LBI open mohawk: the turn.

RFI to LBI open mohawk: after the turn—the check.

Change of edge (RFO to RFI): the starting edge.

Change of edge (RFO to RFI): the free leg extended.

side edge and *scrape* over to the inside edge. Keep your hips and shoulders level throughout —do not tilt in one direction or another. Keep your lean to the center. As in the three, your preparation must be slow and careful, but the turn itself and the check must be lightning fast. Try to relax and have confidence that you will make a good turn! There are many other versions of open and closed mohawks which appear in the more advanced dances, but this will serve to introduce you to one of the more important elements of figure skating.

CHANGES OF EDGE

The changes of edge are moves that take you from one edge to another on the same foot, trac-

ing an S or *serpentine* shape on the ice. Used in the compulsory figures as well as ice dancing, they are also of interest to the recreational skater as a means of control and a variation on plain edges. They can be done from an outside to an inside edge or vice versa, skating either forward or backward, and do not involve a turn. Tightly controlled body positions allow you to make a change that is short and clean—without wobbles. The one we will describe is from a right forward outside edge to a right forward inside edge (RFO to RFI).

Begin as you would a swing roll, with the right shoulder and hip forward, left leg and hip in back and pressed down. Gradually allow the free left foot to come forward and the shoulders and hips to rotate to neutral position. As you approach the long axis where you will change the

Change of edge (RFO to RFI): the change— free leg brought back.

Change of edge (RFO to RFI): the new edge (note position of free leg).

edge, press your free left shoulder back, keeping your shoulders and hips level. At the axis, slightly straighten your skating knee, bringing your free leg back quickly, and at the same time rocking over to the inside edge and bending your right knee as your body goes into neutral position. As you begin skating on the new inside edge, your shoulders and hips will be square to the tracing, and your free left leg will be just inside the circle.

To go from a right forward inside (RFI) edge to a right forward outside (RFO) edge, again begin as you would a swing roll, bringing the free left leg and right shoulder forward just before the long axis, then gradually bringing the left shoulder forward; at the long axis, bring the free leg back as you straighten and then bend the skating knee, assuming neutral position over

your new skating edge. As with the three turns and mohawks, changes of edge are made possible by the sudden release of weight on your skating foot resulting from flexible knee action plus simultaneous changing of body position.

YOUR FIRST FIGURES

Figures require good body control and the ability to skate on an edge. They are the basis for all skating. This is not to say that an individual cannot advance in certain phases of skating without learning the figures, but they can be an immense help. It is easy to measure your progress and—as you learn to control your body in this new way—you will find that you have better control of all your skating. Although the figures require time, concentration, and patience, many people find them very enjoyable.

Instruction is necessary as you begin to learn figures, whether it be group instruction (available at many rinks) or private instruction. With private instruction, you will progress faster since someone familiar with your habits and your personality is watching out for your skating welfare at every point and correcting every error. When availability and expense must be considered, however, group lessons may be a way to get started. Of course, it is also possible to combine group and private instruction—taking one lesson of each every week, for example.

THE BASIC FIGURE EIGHT

All compulsory figures are based on the figure eight, and are usually started on the right foot. A figure may be started either forward or backward and on either an inside or outside edge. Sometimes moves such as a *three turn* are included, and certain of the advanced figures require the skating of three circles or *lobes*. Thus a large number of figures of varying degrees of difficulty are possible. In this book we describe only the first three figures (the easiest), namely the *forward outside circle eight, forward inside circle eight,* and the *waltz eight.*

The basic figure eight is made up of two circles that are tangent to one another. One circle is skated on each foot; then these circles are repeated two more times. As you learned earlier, an imaginary line through the circles, dividing them in half, is called the *long axis.* It is a guide for lining up the circles and any turns that may be made on them.

Crossing the long axis at right angles where the two circles meet is a *short axis* (sometimes called a *transverse axis*). The point where the circles begin is referred to as the *center.* It is here that the skater pushes off, and it is here that the skater later changes to the other foot. Even though it is not in the middle of either circle, it is the center of your figure; if a figure has three circles, there are two centers—one where each circle touches another. On a practice patch, you will find it necessary to move the center or centers every now and then so that you can skate on new ice where your tracings can be seen more easily.

It is recommended that you make the diameter of each of your circles approximately three times your height (loops are an exception, but they are an advanced figure that will not be covered in this book). If you are five feet tall, then your circles should be about fifteen feet across. Now we will introduce you to the figures that are skated in the USFSA Preliminary Test, the forward outside and inside circle eights and the waltz eight.

THE FORWARD OUTSIDE CIRCLE EIGHT

As you stand on the ice preparing to skate this figure, you should be planning it in your head. Try to visualize how large your circles will be on each side of you. How far out will the first quarter extend? (A fifteen-foot circle, for example, always extends seven and a half feet out from the middle of the circle.) Look along your arms to each side to see where your long axis is located. Later, when you are skating tests or competitions, you will be expected to raise your arms in this way before you start—to indicate to the judges where your long axis will be.

Stand in T-position with your back to the middle of the circle you are about to trace. Your shoulders and hips are lined up along the short axis, shoulders level. Keep your head up. Look at the ice ahead of you by moving your eyes, not by bending your head. Your eyes should keep looking at where you want to go, perhaps a quarter of a circle ahead of you. Your skating arm and hand (in this case, the right) will be in front of you over the print you are about to make. Your left arm and hand will be behind you over the print as you make it. Hands should be at about waist level. Weight should be over your left foot at this point, with your ankle turned in.

Remember to push off with the entire side of the blade, not the toe. As you push off, you will leave your left foot behind you in a straight line extending from the hip. The free left foot is turned down and out, with the heel over your tracing. (Have someone check this for you from time to time while you practice.) The left knee is slightly bent. As you skate you will lean toward the middle of your circle with your body moving as a unit, leaning in one line, and with no hips or shoulders sticking out. *Ride the edge —don't try to steer the skate!* Let your edge carry you where it is supposed to go. If your body position is right and you have aimed the edge correctly at the start, you will make a circle. Trying to steer your skate is a bad habit and results in poor form.

Keep this position intact until you reach the one-third point of your circle—or one-half if you can do it. Then gradually bring your free left arm (but not your shoulder) and your free left leg (but not your hip) alongside and pass them in front. They should pass so closely as to *brush* the skating side of your body. It's important to keep the shoulders and hips square to the tracing. The free foot should now reach a position in front of the skating foot with the heel over the tracing you are about to make and the toe pointed down and out. Pointing the free toe not only looks better but helps keep you on your circle and also helps keep your body aligned—so pay attention to this detail.

As you move into the final third of your circle, you will gradually straighten your free left knee until the leg is fully extended in front—but the knee is never locked. You will gradually straighten your skating knee as well. Shoulders and hips remain square to your line of travel. If you've done everything right so far, you can simply coast for the last third of your circle. Look for the center as you come in. About two feet from the center, bring your free foot alongside and take a position with your left arm and hand leading. Now bend your knees, and push off into the left outside circle.

At the push-off, turn the right foot out 90 degrees (a right angle); this will also force you to turn your hips properly. The left skate should take the ice at the center so that the curve it makes joins the one made by your right foot. A slight opening is acceptable, but the lines should not overlap. For your left outside circle, you will follow the instructions given for your right outside circle—just reverse the sides. Working out reverse instructions is a good way to make sure you really understand what you are doing.

If your circles do not return to center, check your starting position to be sure it is held properly. Is your free hip creeping forward? Practice moving the free leg without moving the hip when you are off the ice. Another possible error

is striking out too far—or its opposite, striking so that you cut into your circle. These are the things that will prevent you from making round circles that join nicely.

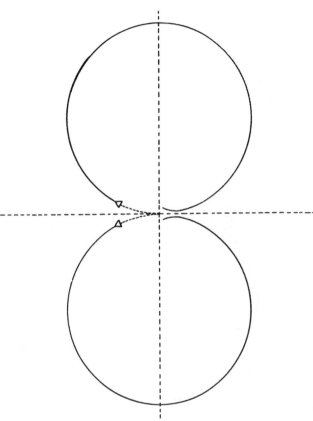

This is what your tracing should look like after you've completed your forward outside circle eight.

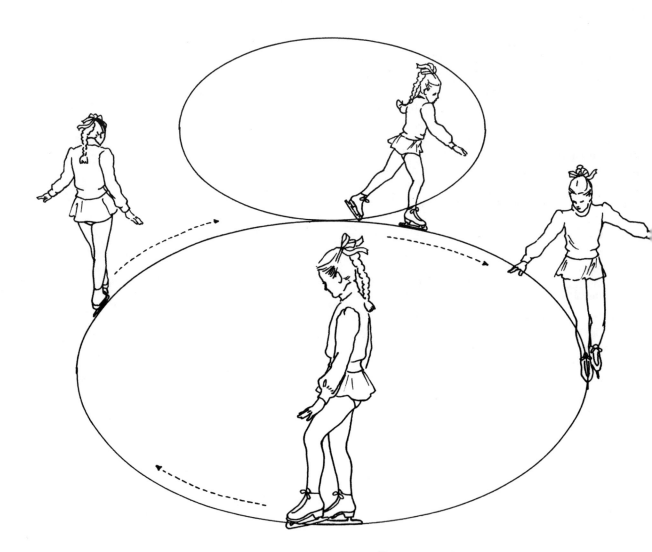

Executing a forward outside circle eight.

Forward outside circle eight: starting position.

Forward outside circle eight: close-up of T-position.

Forward outside circle eight: the push-off onto RFO.

Forward outside circle eight: free foot brushing skating foot.

Forward outside circle eight: free foot extended in front.

Forward outside circle eight: the push-off onto LFO.

THE FORWARD INSIDE CIRCLE EIGHT

Many of the instructions for this figure are the same as for the forward outside circle eight, so read them over again. You will begin with the T-position, hips and shoulders square. Weight is over your left foot. Your free (left) arm and hand will lead for the first third (or half) of your circle, over the print you are about to make; your right hand will be held back over the print you have made. Avoid lunging forward at push-off. Lean your body as a unit toward the middle of the circle. Your free foot goes back after the push-off and is held inside the tracing with the heel of your boot just over the tracing. Don't let this foot drift outside the circle; the swing this creates will force your track to curve inward. *Having most of the free foot positioned inside the circle sets up a counterbalance to the motion made by the rest of your body.* Let the laws of physics work for you!

During this part of the circle, your hips and shoulders should be square. Be sure your hips are held forward and your weight is balanced just back of the center of your skating blade. You should feel a downward pull on your spine, and you can hold your edge by pressing the skating hip *in*. At the one-third (or halfway) point, gently bring your right arm forward and your left arm back, passing them close to the body, and pass your free left foot forward— again always keeping your shoulders and hips square to the line of travel. As before, slowly straighten your skating knee as your free foot moves forward. Maintain this position until you bring your feet together for the new push-off.

At the center, look down at the ice for a moment to be sure you close your circle. With shoulders and hips still squared and with your new free arm forward, bend your knees and push off once again. As you practice, try to watch how your circles are lining up—especially the first time through—and make adjustments as they are needed.

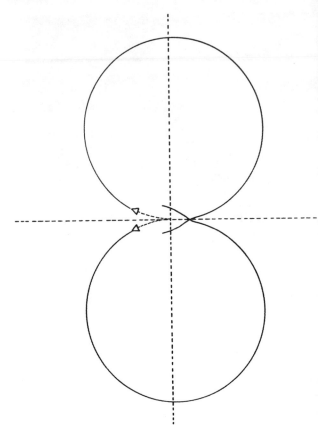

This is what your tracing should look like after you've completed your forward inside circle eight.

Inside circle eight: starting position.

Inside circle eight: the push-off onto RFI (note position of free foot).

Inside circle eight: free foot extended in front.

Inside circle eight: the push-off onto LFI.

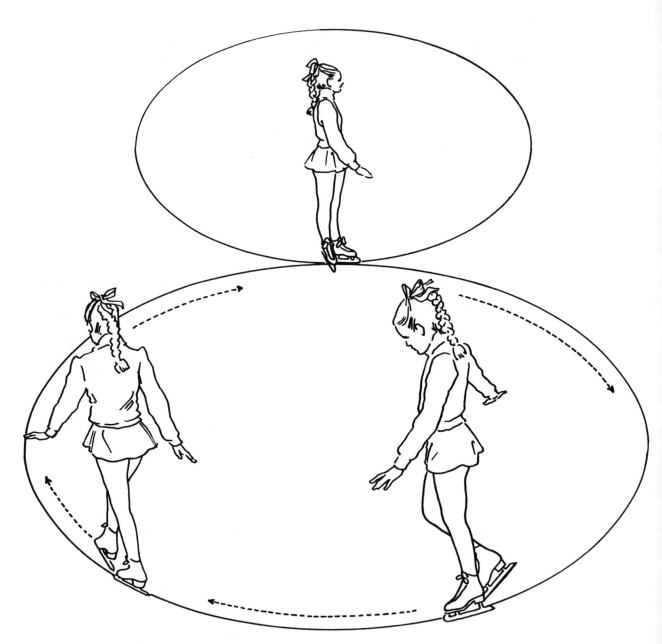

Executing a forward inside circle eight.

THE WALTZ EIGHT

The waltz eight figure has three sections to each circle: a three turn, a back outside edge, and a forward outside edge. You will change feet twice in each circle. Each section should cover one third of the circle, and some skaters like to count each section *1-2-3-4-5-6* to themselves as they skate.

Beginning in T-position, use the position and push-off described for the forward outside circle eight. Rotate your shoulders right away for the three turn, bringing your left arm and shoulder in front with the free leg behind and the foot pointing down over your tracing. Make the turn on the count of *4;* on *5-6,* you will hold your new back inside edge and bring your free left foot alongside. At the one-third point, strike onto the left back outside edge (LBO), and bring your free right foot in front for the count of *1-2-3.* You are now halfway around your circle. For the *4-5-6* count, look over your right shoulder and pass your free right foot back as you hold your LBO edge.

At the two-thirds point, you will do a back-to-forward turn as learned in Chapter 5. Your skating foot (left, in this case) does a *short* back inside edge at the turn. Bend your knees now, strike a right forward outside (RFO) edge, and slowly bring the new free leg forward. Again, shoulders and hips are square as you coast back to center to complete your six counts.

On the second third of this figure (the back outside edge) you begin with a checked position, facing the circle. Slowly pass the free leg back, with the free arm still forward. *Then* allow your head to turn so that you are looking back over your right shoulder, rotate your body to the right (open position), and strike off on your right foot. If you rotate too soon, you will create swing and "jerk the turn."

The waltz eight: preparation for the three turn.

The waltz eight: the LBO edge (note the checked position).

The waltz eight: stroking onto RFO.

The waltz eight: completing the circle.

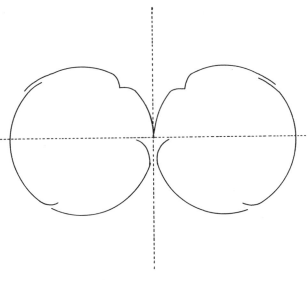

After you've completed your waltz eight, this is what your tracing should look like.

ADVANCED FIGURES

The USFSA Preliminary Test consists of the forward inside and outside circle eights, the waltz eight, and the four skating edges (outside and inside, backward and forward), which have been covered in Chapters 4 and 5. Careful reading of these pages should certainly help qualify you for the Preliminary Test. Beyond the Preliminary Test, you will encounter more difficult figures. There are four types that require one-foot turns done on circles. You have already worked on three turns; on the simplest figure, one three turn is placed on each circle of a figure eight. Turns must be placed on the long axis and must be "clean"—that is, they should not show two lines (which indicate a flat blade) instead of one, or a discontinued line (which shows that the edges have been changed). Judges look for these errors on all types of turns.

Another one-foot turn is the *bracket*. Like the three turn, this involves a turn to an edge of a different character, such as RFO to RBI. The bracket, however, requires rotation in the opposite direction from the three turn, so that the print on the ice will resemble an "inside out" three turn, with the points on the outside of the circle rather than the inside. There are also two one-foot turns that require turning to an edge of the same character, such as RFO to RBO. Both of these require the skating of three circles (*three-lobed figure* is the correct term), with the turns placed where two circles meet. In the *rocker* turn, rotation is in the same direction as in the three turn; in the *counter* turn, rotation is opposite to the three turn, as in the bracket turn.

Some advanced figures require a change of edge where the long axis crosses the center to produce a *serpentine* three-lobed figure. The *loop* figures involve the skating of small loops at the top of each circle of a figure eight. *Paragraph* figures require a skater to skate an entire figure eight on one foot from just one push-off. Since there are three push-offs on each foot, six tracings appear on the ice for a test or competition.

The entire USFSA test structure is set up so that a skater must master the simpler figures before moving on to the more difficult ones. Since figures can be started on either foot, can be skated either forward or backward, and can begin on either an outside or an inside edge, it is obvious that many variations are possible.

9

Ice Dancing

Probably the most popular form of figure skating today is ice dancing. Since being accepted as an Olympic sport in 1976, it has received much added interest from the publicity generated by television. Like pair skating, ice dancing is done by a couple—a man and woman or a boy and girl. Unlike pair skating, emphasis is on the interpretation of various types of dance music and on the skating itself. Partners skate together in specified dance positions and—with only small jumps and lifts permitted—most of the moves are done on the ice. The athletic lifts, jumps, and spins featured in pair skating are seldom seen in ice dancing and then they are used only to achieve a desired effect.

Many younger skaters are now dancing competitively even if their original interest was actually in free skating. The discipline of careful attention to the music and learning to move gracefully with it is beneficial to all skaters. Also, since there are not as many skaters competing in ice dancing (or in pair skating, for that matter), a good partnership can present a better opportunity for skaters to advance than free skating.

Ice dancing is enjoyed by skaters of all ages. Although it is good exercise and requires a limber body, it is not as demanding physically as free skating or pair skating, and older skaters can also excel. The *compulsory dances* are the most common form of ice dancing and can be skated at a rather relaxed pace without long periods of strenuous skating. Adults are generally more familiar with the music prescribed for these dances and will find that the timing and expression come easily to them. Moreover, the sociability that goes with ice dancing is a strong attraction.

Torvill and Dean of Great Britain, 1981 World ice dance champions. (Photo by Cynthia M. Stansfield)

The first dances you will learn are called the *compulsory dances* and are used in competition as well as in tests. They have definite patterns, which can be found in the rulebooks of the USFSA or CFSA as well as in other books. The patterns show exactly where each step must be placed and how many beats of music are required for each step. In ice dancing, of course, the most important thing is *skating in time with the music*. This is crucial. Some skaters who have difficulty in keeping time have improved by taking the dance records or tapes home and walking out the patterns or even by simply listening to the music and picturing the actual skating of the dance patterns in their minds. This also helps them to memorize the pattern at the beginning of each new dance.

As you get into more advanced ice dancing, there will be an opportunity to make your own

selection of dance music and create an original program of *free dance,* just as you would do for a free skating program. Here, too, the timing of your steps to the music must be exact. In your free dance program, you will be required to follow certain rules and will be judged on your general knowledge and ability in dancing as well as your originality in putting together nonrepetitive combinations of new or known dance movements.

Another type of created dance for relatively advanced ice dancers is the *original set pattern* (OSP), in which a couple makes up a series of steps to be placed on the ice surface in a certain way to a prescribed type of music and then repeated either three or six times in three full circuits of the rink. You may have seen these OSP dances on television—for 1981–82 the designated OSP dance music is the *blues*. More freedom is permitted in choice of positions and general content in free dance than in an OSP dance.

Because it is an important part of ice dancing, you should spend as much time as you can listening to good music of all kinds. You will find yourself thinking about moving with it on the ice. Listen to the music as you watch good ice dancers on television or at your local rink. As you progress in ice dancing yourself, you will be using the mohawks, three turns, and swing rolls you have learned. Following are some of the other techniques that you will need in your early compulsory dances.

THE CHASSÉ

The chassé is done in a sequence of three steps, and the free foot is always placed on the ice next to the skating foot. After weight transfer, the free foot is lifted only an inch or so off the ice—straight up—and then replaced alongside to again become the skating foot. Edge sequence is usually outside-inside-outside. Chassés may be done forward or backward. Timing is very precise; for example, when you are skating to waltz music, your chassé sequence might consist of LFO 2 beats, RFI 1 beat, LFO 3 beats.

The *slide* chassé is very similar. After weight transfer, however, the free foot slides off the ice in front of the skating foot and the free leg is held as straight as possible before it is returned alongside to again become the skating foot. The toe of the extended foot is pointed down.

PROGRESSIVES

Progressive steps are similar to the chassé in that they are usually done on outside-inside-outside edges. In this case, however, the second step or stroke passes (progresses) ahead of the skating foot rather than taking the ice alongside. Progressive steps are a means of building up speed in a dance. The idea is always to appear to move effortlessly.

You remember from Chapter 4 that the push must come from the whole side of the blade that is leaving the ice—never from the toe pick. On a left-right-left progressive sequence moving counterclockwise (as most dances do), your first and third steps will get their push in this way, from the inside edge of the right blade as it leaves the ice. These will be strong thrusts. Your second step will be onto the right inside edge, and it must be done with strongly bent knee. As the right foot moves ahead of the left and takes the ice, the left knee is straightened. The push for this second step is provided by the straightening of the left knee and the bending of the right knee. The left foot moves outside the circle rather than straight back, and it leaves the ice only briefly before it is placed on the ice beside the right foot for the third step—which is identical to the first.

Most progressive sequences are made up of three steps. The skating knee is bent for all three. Don't let the skating knee straighten on the middle step or you will appear to be skating with a hobble. When you have smoothed out your forward progressives, begin to work on your backward ones.

SWING ROLLS

Although swing rolls have been described earlier, we must consider them now in the context of ice dancing. Knee action is of primary importance at this point. As your free leg moves from back to forward on a forward swing roll, your skating knee straightens for the forward extension of the swing. Timing for this will depend on your music.

Let's assume you are dancing to waltz music. In that case, the free leg is held back with toe turned out and down and the knee of the skating foot is strongly bent until about the third beat. On the third beat, the skating knee begins to straighten slowly and the free leg swings forward easily. By the fourth beat, the skating knee is straight and the free leg is fully extended forward. It is held there until the sixth beat and then dropped alongside the skating foot. Now both knees bend to start the new stroke, reaching the deepest bend just as you take the new edge. Combined with the rise we have just described at the end of your stroke, this will give an appearance of floating and a smooth action that will be the envy of other ice dancers.

A chassé sequence: the first step (LFO).

A chassé sequence: the chassé (RFI).

A chassé sequence: the third step (LFO).

A slide chassé (LFI).

What we have just described is the knee action or *rise-and-fall* used to express the various types of music you are dancing to. For a waltz, the action builds steadily to a peak and then descends. For a fox-trot, it is smoother with peaks not as high, depths not as low; for blues, you will bend your knees very deeply and stay down much of the time, rising gradually for the longer steps. Knee action gives each dance its unique style and sets ice dancing apart from other aspects of the sport. Swing rolls are, of course, done backward as well as forward and should always be practiced with careful attention to the timing for each dance.

FORWARD CROSS ROLLS

In a cross roll from an outside edge on one foot to an outside edge on the other foot, the free foot is brought *around* the skating foot (it is not picked up and crossed over) and is placed on the ice as the foot leaving the ice makes its thrust. The move is begun with the free foot extended in back; it swings forward and around (so that your legs are crossed above the knees) and takes the ice on an outside edge just as the other foot pushes off. It may be easier to strike the edge in this position if you turn the toe of your striking foot *in* as it takes the ice. The real challenge, however, is in doing all of these things at once without lunging or bending from the waist. You will cross, stroke, and position your new skating blade almost simultaneously. One more hint: if you are having trouble, be sure your free (that is, opposite) hip and shoulder are forward as you make the new stroke.

THE PRELIMINARY DANCES

Together with the skills you have learned in Chapters 4, 5, and 6, the moves we have just described will prepare you for the first three compulsory dances: the Dutch Waltz, the Canasta Tango, and the Swing Dance. The first two require only forward skating, and both partners skate the same steps throughout. Grouped together, these three dances are known as the Preliminary Dances and represent the first level in ice dancing tests and competition. The music you will skate to in each case is specifically

The second step of a progressive sequence (RFI).

An RFO cross roll.

Kilian position.

selected for the style and tempo of the dance and is available through your instructor or skating club.

The Dutch Waltz (skated to waltz music of 138 beats per minute): The pattern for this dance requires one half of the ice rink, beginning at one end and running counterclockwise along that side of the rink and then around the far end. It may be repeated as many times as you wish. You will dance in the *Kilian* position throughout—that is, partners skate in the same direction with the man on the left; the woman's left hand reaches across in front of the man to his left hand; his right shoulder is behind her left shoulder, and their right hands are clasped and held firmly on her right hip. The dance is usually begun at the corner of the rink opposite the corner where you plan to skate the first step.

As many as seven *opening steps* are permitted in any dance, but it is customary to use four more or less straight forward strokes, beginning with the left foot, before you start the Dutch Waltz. They are not used the second time around.

The dance begins with a progressive sequence (LFO 2 beats, RFI 1 beat, LFO 3 beats), followed by a swing roll (RFO 6 beats), another swing roll (LFO 6 beats), and another progressive sequence (RFO 2 beats, LFI 1 beat, RFO 3 beats). As you approach the end of the rink, you will skate one LFO for 3 beats followed by one RFI for 3 beats. Be sure you hold these two steps for their full count. Turning the corner, you will repeat the first four steps of the dance (the left-right-left progressive sequence and the right swing roll). The dance pattern ends with one LFO for 3 beats and one RFI for

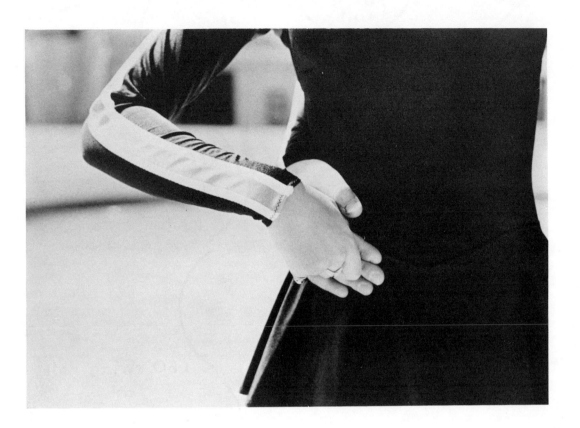

3 beats, and you go directly into your pattern again.

Try to use the rise-and-fall technique we described earlier in this chapter, particularly on the 3-beat and 6-beat edges. You will notice that the progressive sequences are 2-1-3 beats in this dance, designed to fit the rhythm of the waltz. It will take a little work before you and your partner can move smoothly together—doing your steps in perfect unison will come in time as your style improves and you both relax and enjoy your ice dancing.

The Canasta Tango (skated to tango music of 104 beats per minute): As you will see from the diagram, this dance also follows a simple counterclockwise pattern. It is danced in *reverse Kilian* position, with the man on the right of the woman and their left hands clasped on her left hip. Opening steps are the same as for the Dutch Waltz, four forward strokes beginning on the left foot.

The Canasta Tango begins with a progressive sequence (LFO 1 beat, RFI 1 beat, LFO 1 beat), followed immediately by a chassé (RFI 1 beat). This is actually the *second* step of the chassé sequence you have been practicing; the first is the final step of the introductory progressive sequence. It is followed by a 4-beat LFO swing roll, which is also the last step of your chassé sequence. Now you do a slide chassé (RFO 2 beats, LFI 2 beats), with the next step held as a swing roll (RFO 4 beats). Another slide chassé follows (LFO 2 beats, RFI 2 beats), and a progressive sequence (LFO 1 beat, RFI 1 beat, LFO 2 beats). The pattern of this dance ends with a 4-beat RFO swing roll

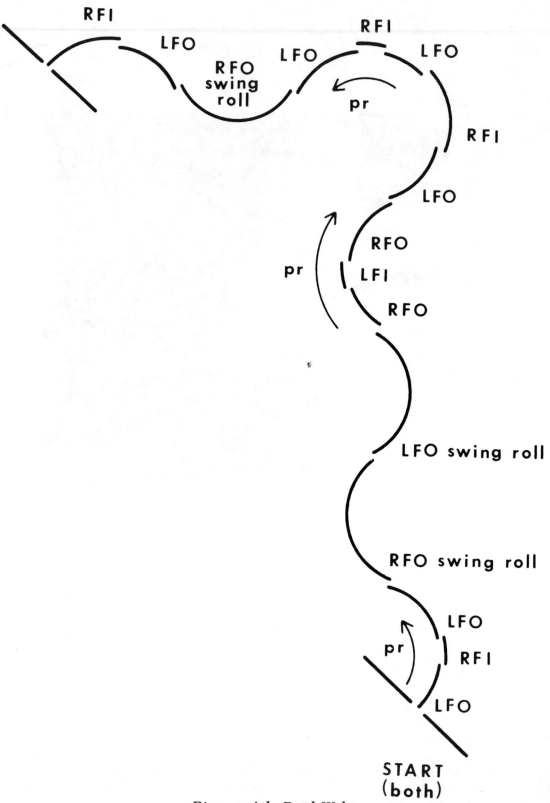

RFI

LFO

RFO
swing
roll

RFI

LFO

LFO

pr

RFI

LFO

RFO

pr

LFI

RFO

LFO swing roll

RFO swing roll

LFO

pr

RFI

LFO

START
(both)

Diagram of the Dutch Waltz.

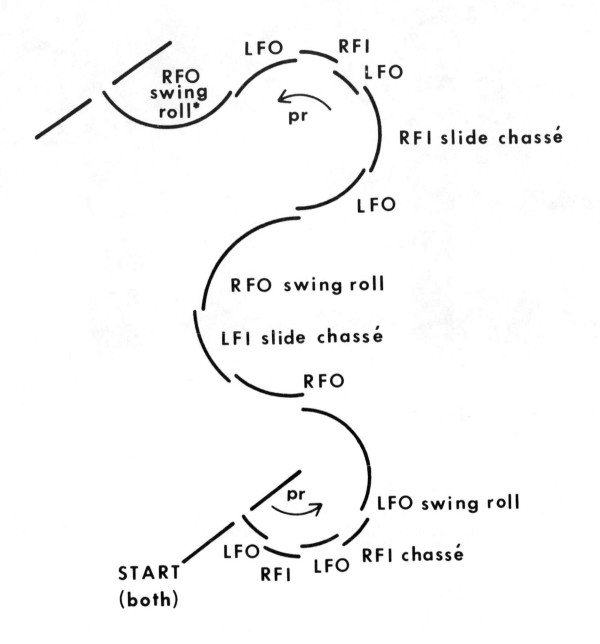

LFO   RFI

RFO swing roll*

LFO

pr

RFI slide chassé

LFO

RFO swing roll

LFI slide chassé

RFO

pr

LFO swing roll

LFO

RFI chassé

LFO

RFI

START (both)

*Optional RFO cross roll

Diagram of the Canasta Tango.

Closed position.

that may be done optionally as a cross roll (partners should agree on this in advance).

You will notice that the middle lobe of this dance pattern—the first slide chassé—reaches to the center of the rink. Five extensions of the free leg are required, and these should express tango style. The free leg is held back until the last moment and moves forward to full extension at approximately the third beat. Be sure the toe is pointed down. This move should be crisp, but it is not a kick.

The Swing Dance (skated to fox-trot music of 96 beats per minute): This is the first dance to include turns and backward skating. Each partner skates backward for half of the pattern. Partners actually do skate the same steps in this dance, but not at the same time. New dance

movements include backward chassé sequences, backward swing rolls, and a *dropped* three turn, in which the edge after the turn is held briefly and the weight then transferred (or dropped) to the free foot.

The principal position for this dance is *closed* (sometimes called *waltz*) position, in which the partners face each other with the man's right hand placed just below the woman's right shoulder blade. His elbow should bend sufficiently to keep the couple close. The woman's left hand is pressed firmly against the man's right shoulder, and her elbow rests on his. Her right hand and the man's left hand (the *lead* hands) are clasped and extended at a mutually comfortable height and should not waver up and down or in and out. While the partners are skating in *hand-*

Hand-in-hand position.

in-hand position, the one who has turned from back to forward should skate to the inside of the circle they are making and leave enough room for the other—but they should never be so far apart that lunging or bending is needed to complete their moves.

Opening steps for the Swing Dance are usually begun in the corner of the rink with the woman on the man's left side in hand-in-hand position. One way is for both partners to do a 4-beat LFO swing roll; then the man does a 4-beat RFO swing roll while the woman does a RFO dropped three turn (turning on the second beat) to face him. Going into closed position, the couple begins the dance pattern with a chassé sequence (*Man:* LFO 1 beat, RFI 1 beat, LFO 2 beats; *Woman:* RBO 1 beat, LBI 1 beat, RBO 2 beats). A second chassé sequence follows (*Man:* RFO 1 beat, LFI 1 beat, RFO 2 beats; *Woman:* LBO 1 beat, RBI 1 beat, LBO 2 beats). This is followed by two 4-beat swing rolls, LFO and RFO for the man, RBO and LBO for the woman.

In the end pattern, the partners do a series of six 2-beat edges, with the woman making a simple counterclockwise turn from back to front into hand-in-hand position (RBO-LFO-RFI-LFO-RFI-LFO), and the man doing any type of forward inside mohawk into closed position (LFO-RFI-LFO-RFI-LBI-RBO). A 4-beat swing roll (LBO for the man, RFO for the woman) completes the first half of the pattern, and it is now repeated with the woman skating forward and the man backward.

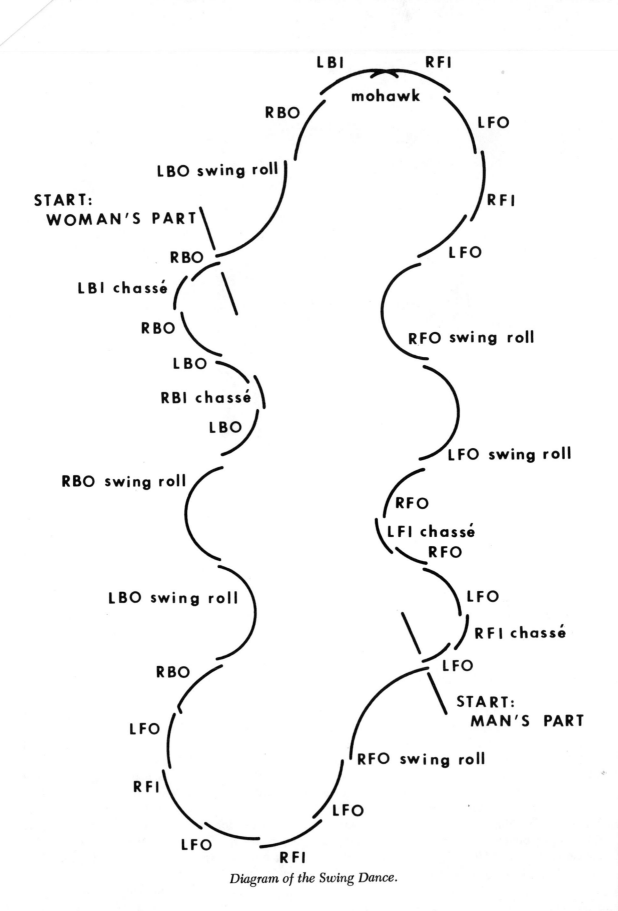

Diagram of the Swing Dance.

10

Free Skating

In this chapter, we describe some of the fundamental moves of free skating as well as a few that are more difficult. Spirals, pivots, spins, and some of the simple jumps can be learned by nearly everyone—in time. Advanced jumps require good coaching. What you must remember always is to master the beginning moves completely before you try to build on them with more complicated moves. If you are working with a coach who uses a different approach on a particular move, you will, of course, want to do exactly what your coach tells you to do. The instruction we give is in common use, however, and it can be helpful at times to think through a move from another point of view. Descriptions of more advanced jumps, such as the split, the axel, and the lutz, are included here primarily to give you an idea of what lies ahead and to help you better appreciate free skating competition

on television or wherever you may see it. The USFSA Preliminary Test, for example, requires a waltz jump, a toe loop, a salchow, a half flip (or half lutz), a one-foot spin, and a two-foot spin—and many skaters find that it is somewhat easier to pass than the Preliminary Test in compulsory figures or in ice dancing.

SPIRALS

A spiral is a long, gliding edge usually done in a position that resembles a ballet dancer's *arabesque*. If held for an extended period of time, the edge would trace a circular pattern in which the circles become smaller and smaller. In *spiral position*, the trunk should be horizontal with the back strongly arched; the free leg is extended straight behind the body with the foot usually

Spiral position (RFO).

A Charlotte death spiral by Riegel and Nisch-
witz of West Germany, 1981 World bronze
medalists in pair skating. (Photo by Cynthia M.
Stansfield)

A simple inside forward spiral.

held at the same height as the head. Head and shoulders are up, with arms extended so that hands are at shoulder level. The beauty of the spiral derives from its flow and grace—the arch of the back combined with the curve presented by head, arms, and free leg.

Spirals can be skated on either foot, forward or backward, on each edge, and with a wide variety of arm positions. In the *Colledge spiral* (named after Cecilia Colledge, who was recently elected to the USFSA Hall of Fame), the free leg is elevated to a nearly vertical position while the body remains horizontal. The *Charlotte spiral* (named after Charlotte Oelschlagel, whom you met in the first chapter) has a much lower body position combined with the very high free leg. A version of this, done with a partner in pair skating, is commonly known as the *death spiral*. It is also possible to bring the free leg from behind to the side and then forward.

With the spiral, you will try for as many positions as you can master—but the first thing is to learn the basic position and the balance that goes with it. To begin with, you can practice off the ice or standing at the barrier holding on with both hands. Stretch the free leg behind, with your knee straight and your toe up and

out. You will gradually be able to stretch it higher and longer with practice. Your trunk is horizontal and your back is arched as much as you can manage. Never look down. Your head is looking forward. For a forward spiral, your heel will be pressed into the ice for balance. To be too far forward on the blade is to court disaster —you can fall on your face. When you feel ready, bring your arms out at the sides in a curved position, with hands curving up from the wrists.

After you get a feel for the position, try it on a shallow edge. Begin on two feet, gradually raising your free leg and lowering your body from the hips. Try to straighten both knees as much as you can, right from the start. You will want someone to watch you and tell you whether your body lines are straight and your back sufficiently arched. Now slowly deepen your edge as you work to perfect your spiral position.

Many skaters very often use the inside forward spiral, sometimes called the *Hayes Jenkins spiral* for the Olympic champion who popularized it. If this is to be done on a left forward inside edge, the right arm goes forward and the left arm goes back. You will need a deep bend of the left knee. The right foot is brought forward from in back and held (as in a crossover) outside the left foot and parallel to it, very close to the ice. Some skaters learn to lean forward enough from this position so as to touch the ice with the right hand. This is a spiral that can also be done backward, and some skaters can even turn from forward to back while in the spiral position.

SPREAD EAGLES

Just as the name implies, this move is done with your hips pressed back and your feet pointing in opposite directions but holding the same edge, either outside or inside. It can be skated on clockwise or counterclockwise curves, which can be joined, or it can be skated nearly in a straight line. Spread eagles are much more difficult for some of us than for others. You may need to practice limbering up off the ice in order to get your feet to turn out more easily, and there are some people who will never look good—or feel good—doing spread eagles.

One way to begin is at the barrier. With your

An outside spread eagle.

An inside spread eagle.

feet near the boards and your hands on the rail, bring your feet as close together as you can with heels in and toes out so that they are almost parallel to the boards. Bend your knees and turn your ankles until you are on the outside edges of your blades. Now straighten your knees and tuck in your hips and buttocks, but leave your ankles dropped. Push yourself along the barrier for a while, holding your outside edges and keeping your knees as straight as possible.

Another approach is to start gliding forward on a left outside edge, swing your right leg forward and then back to a heel-to-heel position and a back outside edge. (Many beginners do an outside spread eagle from this kind of start.) With either method, keep your right hand in front of your body when you are traveling to the left, your left arm stretching ahead of you. Your body will twist slightly to the left. Stand straight with hips in, head held back and looking along your line of travel. Never look down! Pull up on your diaphragm, and keep your heels as close together as you can.

Still another way of getting into this move is to start by gliding with both feet on the ice. Move one skate in front of the other; now flip the other around behind it. Once you have it, be sure to learn the spread eagle in both directions and on inside edges as well as outside. The more you can do them, the easier they become; doing them repeatedly will eventually make you more limber. On inside spread eagles, shallow edges are more difficult; if they are too deep, however, you will trace a small circle. Done

A spread eagle variation known as the Ina Bauer.

think it provides the best over-all picture of a pivot.

As you are skating a short, slow curve on your right back outside edge, bend both knees and place your free left arm in front. Swing your free foot inside the circle, well behind your skating foot and toward the center of the curve you are making. Drag the pick lightly over the surface for a short distance; when you have slowed down sufficiently, jab the point straight down into the ice. The left knee should be kept inside your curve. Now turn your right heel out and shift most of your weight to the left toe pick, pulling your left shoulder back hard and also your head. Your right skate remains on the ice and on its RBO edge, making a small circle around the implanted toe pick. Once you learn to do it, many revolutions are possible before you come to a stop. A pivot like this makes a good ending to a sequence or to a program of free skating.

The forward inside pivot is much easier. Begin as though you were going to do an inside mohawk; as you make your curve smaller, stretch your free foot inside the circle—with the free arm back and the skating arm forward as in the mohawk. Now drag your pick, implant it, put weight on it, bend the knee over it, and let the other skate pivot in a circle around it. In all pivots, let the pick take hold slowly so that you form a smaller and smaller circle. After a while, you will be able to enter a pivot skating backward at a good speed and gradually bring yourself to a stop.

properly, your lean on inside spread eagles will be from the edge of the blade without the ankles dropped.

Another version of the spread eagle is the *Ina Bauer*, which is done on the inside edge of one foot and the outside edge of the other. The feet are turned out as in a spread eagle, but are not directly in line with each other.

PIVOTS

In a pivot, one of your toe picks is dug into the ice as you make small circles around it with your other blade. We will describe first a pivot beginning on a right back outside edge. Although this is not the easiest one to learn, we

SPINS

As you have been told before, the most important thing in skating is balance! This is certainly never more true than in spinning. We can't tell you a great deal about spins—they can only be learned by *doing*. Like feeling your way along a dark passage, you gradually will do it more efficiently and with greater speed. Although you have to learn it by yourself, we will try to provide a little light along the passage to the world of spins.

The first thing you can expect is to encounter a certain amount of dizziness. Your body is not used to this motion and has to adjust, just as

Starting an RBO pivot.

Turning an RBO pivot.

Completing an RBO pivot.

Starting an RFI pivot.

sailors learn to adjust to the wave motion at sea. It may take time, but there are some suggestions we can offer to help: Look straight ahead—not up, not down, nor to the sides. Don't pick out a spot to watch and twist your head around the way a ballerina does. Let your head move with your body. Then, when you stop, jab the toe of your free foot into the ice to make the stop sudden, and at the same time toss your head back in the direction from which you have come—just as if you were tossing the hair out of your eyes. This will help clear up the dizziness.

Another difficulty encountered in spins is *travel*. You must learn to center your spin so that it stays in one spot and does not move over the surface of the ice. Unlike most skating movements, spinning requires a straight knee. If your knee is not straight, you will travel; so, when you think you are spinning on a straight knee, straighten it a bit more. Your shoulders, of course, should always be level and your body straight.

When it comes to spins and jumps, we all have a preferred natural direction of rotation, some to the right (clockwise), and some to the left (counterclockwise). Some coaches will recommend that you learn to spin only in your natural direction (they can tell you which way that is), and they will say the same about jumping. It is becoming increasingly common, however, to learn to spin—and even to jump—on either foot. For one thing, you will be learning change-foot spins as you progress. These will undoubtedly be easier for you if you have begun by learning to spin on either foot. In addition, knowing how to spin and jump in either direction allows you more variety when you are planning a free skating program for performance. If, for some reason, you do decide to learn to spin and jump in one direction only, it should certainly be in the same direction for both. Again, this is to improve your program options. Most skaters actually do prefer to spin counterclockwise (to the left), and that is the direction we will describe.

The easiest spin is the *two-foot spin*. Done on the blades, rather than on the toe pick, it is begun with both feet on the ice about twelve inches apart. Since you will spin to the left, you must first shift your weight and throw your arms and shoulders to the right; then swing quickly to the left, following through with your back arm

One way to start a two-foot spin.

A two-foot spin.

A one-foot spin.

to propel your body into a left spin. Spinning counterclockwise, you will have the weight on the ball of your left foot and the heel of your right. As you begin to spin, you will gain speed by bringing your arms in close to your body.

This spin can also be started by placing most of your weight on your left foot and gliding straight ahead on flat blades—then pulling in your arms and spinning as described above. A third way is to glide forward in a counterclockwise curve with both feet on the ice (a left outside and a right inside edge); skate a large circle with your right foot, shift your weight to the left foot, bend your left knee, and make the circle smaller. Your right foot will be well back. When the circle becomes quite small, swing your right foot around and even with the left—

and *spin*. Straighten both knees and pull in your arms as you begin spinning.

A *one-foot spin* may be done simply by picking up one foot during a two-foot spin, but a really good one will begin with an approach that builds up your speed and rotation. So that we can include a few more words about the problem of travel, we will describe a one-foot spin done on the blades rather than the easier one done on the toe pick and usually called a *scratch spin*.

A one-foot spin on your blade may begin with an RFO three turn; then you skate an LBO edge and do a back crossover onto a deep RBI edge. Arms and shoulders should be checked, facing the circle, with your head looking back. Now go forward onto a left outside edge with a very

deep knee bend. Press your hip into the circle with your skating arm forward. Don't reach. Your right foot should swing in a wide arc, and your free arm swings around with it. As your left edge deepens, you will find yourself spinning to the left. Now bring your free leg forward, straighten your skating (spinning) knee, and find your balance by shifting your weight toward the toe of your skate. Bring your free foot up to the skating knee with arms held at the sides. For speed, bring your free foot in front, lower it, and pull your arms in.

After completing your spin with either the "jab and toss" we described earlier or a step onto a back outside edge with your free foot, go back and look at the print you have made. You will see a three turn before the spin; this is where you should have begun to straighten and spin. Your spin will show a larger circle, then smaller ringlets within it if it was done correctly. It is more likely that you will see one or more loops progressing over the surface of the ice—like the wandering path of a wobbling top. Like the top, you had begun to travel because you were out of balance.

It takes time to learn your spins. The more you learn to center your spins, the more revolutions you will be able to do. Two or three times around is a good beginning—particularly if you don't travel a lot. If your circles have two lines (one deeper than the other), this indicates you have used your first toe pick as well as your blade. As we told you, scratch spins are done on this pick—and they are easier to learn, even

A "jab and toss" stop.

though we recommend learning to spin first on your blade.

SIT SPINS

Once you have learned to control your spins, you will probably want to try the *sit* spin (also called a *Jackson Haines* after its inventor). One clear advantage to learning this spin is that you have a smaller distance to go if you should fall! You can practice a sit spin first in a chair or on a bench. Your upper body will lean forward from the waist slightly but in a single line. Your free foot should be straight out in front of you, its heel level with your seat. Hold the boot of the free foot in both hands while you press down on the free knee with the elbow on the same side to keep the toe turned out.

On the ice, you will use the same approach as for the one-foot spin. Lean your body forward, and swing your free foot around (from high in back to low in front) as your spin begins. Deepen your knee bend quickly. Your hands should be extended in front waiting for the free foot. If you have trouble getting up again, press down with your arms on the skating knee—the way many people help themselves up out of a chair by pressing their palms down on their thighs.

Starting a sit spin.

A sit spin.

JUMPING

In all jumps, position is very important. If your body is kept upright and properly aligned, you are less likely to fall than if your position collapses. Your feet will be under you—where they belong. Even if you do not land your jump on the intended edge, your blades will touch the ice first, and you can probably get one or the other blade down in time to save your balance. Position is also important for appearance. Doing a jump so that it looks like something special is, after all, the whole idea. Even a missed jump doesn't look too bad if the form is good. On the other hand, you may be able to land on the correct edge with bad form—but it won't look good to anyone.

Your spring and "hang time" come from a well-bent skating knee. *Think of your knee as a coiled spring that will release the needed energy for your jump.* If it is not sufficiently bent, it has little power to give you. Contrary to what most non-skaters believe, jumps are easier when done with speed. *Speed contributes to the height and distance of your jump, and these—in turn—give you more time to rotate and set up your landing.*

Practically all jumps require rotation of the skater's body in the air, ranging from half a revolution in the case of the waltz jump to three complete revolutions in the case of the triple jumps. This rotational force is provided by the action of the arms and free leg as the skater goes into the jump. Once in the air, the arms may be brought close to the body to make rotation even faster. This is of real concern in the case of double and triple jumps, where only a limited time is available to complete the required revolutions.

On landing a jump, the skater must check rotation to avoid a two-foot landing or even a fall on the ice. *Arms, hips, and shoulders should always be square to the landing foot at the moment of impact.* The head should be in line with the body, looking directly forward. If your head turns or if you look over your shoulder, your landing foot will curve inward—and you will probably go off your edge. It is true that some coaches recommend landing with the free arm forward; this may be somewhat easier for beginners, but serious skaters should learn the correct position from the start since it is the basic land-

The bunny hop.

ing position for all advanced and combination jumps.

Every jump has its own "rhythm." You will acquire a feeling about being set for takeoff, about the amount of time you are in mid-air, and a sense of your body position on landing. This is particularly true for multiple-revolution jumps, and it comes to you only from doing the jump over and over. Once you have it down pat (again, like riding a bicycle), you can return to that jump with confidence and know what to expect of your body.

It is probably a good idea to practice jumps off the ice as well as on. Rotation and alignment may be improved by practicing on a trampoline, for example, where you will not have to think about takeoff or landing. Jumping on a floor will give you good traction for takeoff and landing practice, but don't forget what we said about

The waltz jump: preparation.

The waltz jump: going into the jump.

the importance of speed. Most of your practice will always be on the ice, and it won't be long before you appreciate the importance of good coaching.

THE BUNNY HOP

Undoubtedly the easiest jump, since it requires no turning in the air, is the bunny hop. This is a good starter, just a simple forward leap from the flat blade of one foot to the toe pick of the other foot and then onto the flat blade of the skating foot. To take off from your left foot, start with your left knee deeply bent and your free right leg in back. Spring straight up from the left blade, using your knee for a spring. After you leave the ice, kick your left leg back and swing

your right leg straight forward. Keep it straight, and then bend your right knee to cushion your landing on the toe pick. Now push off from the pick to the flat blade of your left skate. You should practice this jump from your right foot as well.

THE WALTZ JUMP

The waltz jump is done from a forward outside edge on one foot to a back outside edge on the other, with a half revolution in mid-air. We will describe it from LFO to RBO. A good way to go into this jump is from a right back outside edge with some speed. Bring your free left leg back to the right heel as you look back over your left shoulder. Left shoulder and hip are checked.

The waltz jump: at the height of the jump.

The waltz jump: landing (note checked position).

You will turn forward, changing briefly to a left forward outside edge with deeply bent knee (to give you spring) and stretching back with your free right arm and leg. As you leave the ice, your free right leg and both arms are thrust upward simultaneously—with the free leg aimed outside the curve you are on. As you jump, the left leg straightens and follows the free arm and shoulder. The left shoulder leads as in a three turn. Breathe in as you take off. Now allow your shoulders to follow the swing of your free leg—this will give you a *held* revolution of 180 degrees, one of the requirements of the waltz jump.

As your jump reaches its highest point, shift your weight to the right side so that you will land over the front of your right blade (but *not* on the toe pick). Your right knee is slightly bent

as you land and bends more deeply on impact; then it straightens when your new edge is under control. You should be looking straight ahead, with arms (now extended to the sides), shoulders, and hips square to your line of travel. The waltz jump is an easy jump—one of the first you will learn—but with techniques that will serve you well as you advance into the more sophisticated jumps.

THE THREE JUMP

The three jump is very similar to the waltz jump. Beginning on a left forward outside edge, jump from a bent knee. Swing your right leg up and forward, close to the jumping leg. Turn it out and press it back as in a three turn. You will

The three jump: landing on LBI edge.

The half flip: takeoff.

land on your left back inside edge, using the same checked position as for a three turn. The real beauty of the three jump lies in making the jump seem to *float*.

SOME TOE JUMPS

Jumps can be done straight from an edge or from an edge with an assist from the toe pick of the free foot. In toe jumps, the pick serves as a fulcrum to support the jump while the bent skating knee serves to provide the power. To get the feeling of jumping from your toe picks, you might try simply jumping up and down—jabbing the picks firmly and quickly into the ice—first on both feet and then alternating. When you do these jumps, you will place the

pick in the ice as you snap your bent (skating) knee straight for the takeoff. You will feel your legs actually pulling toward each other.

FLIPS

The *half* flip begins on a back inside edge that can be approached by turning an inside mohawk. Since you are jumping counterclockwise, your right arm and shoulder are held back in the checked position normally entered after a mohawk and your left arm and shoulder are forward. Keep your back straight and your left knee bent. Sight along your forward arm, keeping your hips forward and square. Stretch your right leg back with the knee straight, kneecap *down* and a few inches above the ice. As you

The half flip: in mid-air—the turn.

The ballet jump.

place the toe pick in the ice, your body should begin turning a half revolution. You will land as for a bunny hop—lightly on your left toe pick—and then skate off on a right forward inside edge.

To do a *full*-revolution flip, you will move your left shoulder back and your right shoulder forward as you take off. After a full (360-degree) revolution, you will land as you did for the waltz jump.

THE BALLET JUMP

The beauty of this jump is in its stretched position, and all your effort should go into creating a nice picture with good form. Ballet jumps are done from a back outside edge. Stretch the free

leg back and begin to turn your shoulders as you do so. As you pick, bend your left knee and jump straight up. Lift the right leg, turning the knee out and pointing the toe down and out. Your left leg is slightly forward and should be stretched downward. You will land on the left pick and skate forward on a right forward inside edge.

THE STAG JUMP

This is a variation on the ballet jump. The difference lies in the position of the left leg. For a stag jump, instead of holding the leg straight down, you bend the left knee forward while the right leg is extended in back. It is possible to use a *stag variation* on many other jumps: sim-

The mazurka.

The toe loop: takeoff.

ply bend the knee of the forward leg as we have described here.

THE MAZURKA

Although similar to the ballet jump, the mazurka requires crossing your legs in mid-air. Taking off from a right back outside edge, you will cross your right toe in front of your left. After completing a half turn, you will land on the right toe pick and skate off on your left forward outside edge.

THE TOE LOOP

This is a one-revolution jump done from the same right back outside edge as the ballet jump.

With shoulders turning left, place your left pick in the ice and—with no hesitation—do a waltz jump off the toe. If you open your free shoulder as described, it will seem at first more like a half-revolution jump; however, it is jumped from a back outside edge to the same back outside edge, and you should gradually do it from a more closed position.

THE TOE WALLEY

Somewhat similar to the toe loop, the toe walley begins on a back inside edge. It, too, lands on the same foot—but on a back outside edge. To make this possible, although your rotation will be into the circle as in the toe loop, you will be rotating a little farther because of the inside

The toe loop: landing.

touches the ice first, and then you take a right forward inside edge.

For this jump to look good, you must have perfect form,—with body erect and with legs as nearly parallel to the ice as you can get them (you can work on this off the ice). Split jumps may also be done with a full revolution; the last half revolution comes after the split, and you will land on your back edge. A *Russian* split is similar, but the hands touch the feet.

MORE EDGE JUMPS—THE LOOP JUMP

Known in Europe as the *Rittberger,* after its inventor, the loop jump is done from a back outside edge to the same edge after one revolution. A good approach is a right forward inside three turn into a deep back outside edge with a strong closed check. If this is uncomfortable for you, you can try a left forward outside three turn to a right back outside edge. In either case, the closed position is essential to learning this jump, and you must not open up as you would for a toe loop or toe walley. The depth of your edge and inward rotation are going to supply about all of the rotation you will need. Once you have reached this point, you can concentrate mostly on your jumping. Jump straight up by straightening your skating knee (the right, in this case), and swing your left leg up and around the right leg so that your legs are actually crossed. As you jump, your left arm swings back and the right arm swings forward. Be sure to keep your body straight. You will land as for a waltz jump.

edge takeoff. As you jump, keep your feet close together in the air. Try for height and continued speed from takeoff through landing. It will help your rotation to think of bringing your right shoulder all the way around.

THE SPLIT JUMP

This is actually a half flip done in a split position. As you jump, bring your feet together. Then kick your left leg forward and your right leg straight back from the hip. Your left arm is brought across your body as it turns forward, and your right arm is flung back. Allow yourself to remain in split position as long as you can. Don't try to bring your left foot down until your body begins to descend. The left toe pick

THE HALF LOOP JUMP

In spite of its name, this is actually a full-revolution jump. You begin it like a loop jump from a back outside edge, but you land on the back inside edge of the opposite foot. The free leg remains crossed in front of the jumping leg at takeoff. Partway through the jump the free leg reaches out for the landing, and the strongly checked position is assumed as in the case of the waltz jump.

The split jump.

A Russian split.

Taking off for the loop jump.

THE WALLEY JUMP

Although the walley was originated by Englishman Pat Low, it is named after Nathan Wally who first introduced it in the United States. (The accepted official spelling today is *walley*.) It is made from the back inside edge of one foot to the back outside edge of the same foot, and it is very effective if done with speed and height. A common approach is from a left back inside edge with the free leg behind. You *hop* to a right back inside edge and, with a deep bend of your right knee and your new free leg behind, you spring almost immediately. Swing your left foot back around the right foot, turning the knee and hip out as you jump. The left shoulder turns out, and the right follows it as you complete the jump. Keep your feet close together while in the air, and land on a right back outside edge, as in a waltz jump.

THE SALCHOW

Named after the great Swedish skater Ulrich Salchow, this is a jump from a back inside edge to a back outside edge on the opposite foot. It is one of the easiest single-revolution jumps, and is also a fairly easy double-revolution jump. Rotation is easy; in fact, it is hard to check the rotation. Gaining good height on the jump is not so easy. The secret lies in the application of pressure at the right point on takeoff and in a good check position being set up for landing. The most common approaches are from an inside mohawk or from a forward outside three turn. We will describe the jump from a left outside three turn.

After turning the three, hold the position briefly. It should be the same as it was for the flip jump—free side open and back, skating shoulder and hip held forward and closed, head sighting along the skating shoulder. Once you have set this position following the three turn, deepen your edge and your knee bend, making sure your skating hip is turned inward toward the circle. Swing your free leg (the right) in a wide arc with a sweeping motion around the skating foot and spring from the left foot, jumping off the *heel* of the skate, not the toe. The pressure at takeoff will come in the ankle. As you jump, your right arm and shoulder will follow the free leg around. Land as you did for a waltz jump, but initially with a strong check of the shoulder and hip on the free side. Try to keep your back straight from takeoff to landing.

If you jump off the toe, you will make a scraping sound and leave a telltale gouge in the ice. Doing the salchow jump this way will make it more difficult as you attempt doubles or triples. The pressure and the timing are keys to improving your salchow. Since the jump is fairly easy, we recommend strongly that you spend time on these aspects while you are learning the single salchow.

THE LUTZ

Probably the most difficult of the one-revolution jumps, the lutz is similar to the flip except that

The salchow: takeoff.

The salchow: in the air.

it begins from a back outside edge. Because the blade at this point is tracing a curve in a direction opposite to the rotation of the jump itself, you must first position yourself as if you were going one way and then suddenly go the other way. This causes a tendency to change to an inside edge. Takeoff is assisted by the toe pick. You will land on the back outside edge of the other foot. (For a half lutz, you would land on the toe pick of the jumping foot and then skate off on the forward inside edge of the other foot.)

THE AXEL

Named after its inventor, Axel Paulsen of Norway, the axel jump is a one-and-a-half-revolu-

tion jump from a forward outside edge to a back outside edge of the opposite foot. It is really just a combination of the waltz jump and the single loop jump. Starting off in the position of the waltz jump, the skater must turn backward into loop jump position while in mid-air. Not surprisingly, there are skaters who find a double flip or a double salchow far easier than a single axel.

The approach for an axel is the same as that for a waltz jump. Skate a right back outside edge, and bring your free left leg back to the right heel with left shoulder and hip checked. Look back over your left shoulder. Step forward on your left outside edge with a strongly bent knee, left shoulder leading and right arm and leg well back. As you spring into the air, your free right arm and leg are thrust strongly forward and upward to give height and rotation to

Landing an axel.

the jump. During the last revolution, arms are held close to the body and legs are crossed in front as in the loop jump.

FREE SKATING COMPETITION

When you have learned to jump well, you can incorporate your jumps with your spins and other free skating moves to develop a program of your own. You will find that skating competition is probably the most exciting part of the sport. As you see yourself improve, you will quite naturally begin to set goals for yourself. Some will be short-range goals that are just up the road and can realistically be achieved; others are more in the realm of dreams, achievements you would like to reach someday—if.

Whether or not you do will depend on how much you want them, your own talent, the kind of instruction you get, how much time and money you can spend, and many other things (including, very possibly, a bit of luck).

Most such dreams include competition. There are many levels of competition. When you can do some of the jumps and spins described in this chapter, and do them fairly well, you will probably be thinking about competing at a lower level. You will learn that there are competitions in figures, free skating, pairs, and ice dancing. At the top of the list are the *qualifying* competitions, by which skaters advance to National, World, and (every four years) Olympic championships. Most skaters, however, begin in either *non-qualifying* or *club* competitions. Club competitions are held for members of a particular club; non-qualifying events are usually open to all registered USFSA amateurs, or at least to those from a particular state or region. Within each of these are categories for skaters of varying levels, and—as mentioned earlier—your eligibility for each group depends on the number of tests you have passed. Some are open to skaters who have passed no tests, and there are also competitions for those working on the elementary badge or ribbon programs.

When you become a competitor, you are entering the mainstream of figure skating. You get to know people from other clubs and rinks, to gauge your skills against other skaters, and also to see at firsthand some very good skating. Let's assume that you are thinking of entering non-qualifying competitions at a low level in free skating, the route followed by most skaters today. The first thing you will need is a program.

YOUR FREE SKATING PROGRAM

The program is a planned pattern for your free skating routine. It is developed around a piece of music (on a record or tape) and, like any other performance, must be learned and perfected. Probably the most important step is the selection of your music. Since free skating is intended to express music, you will want to select music with which you are comfortable, which you can *enjoy,* and which has highlights that match the kind of skating you do. Skaters often make certain mistakes in choosing their music: they try to use something that serves as only *background* music—something with few highlights or changes—which they can pretty much ignore; or they select music that is too hard for them to express. As a beginning free skating competitor, you will want music that is not too demanding, music with some clear highlights but not too many, and with a tempo you can keep up with easily. Something light and easily understood makes a good choice for the new free skater.

Your coach will, of course, be helping you choose your music. Depending on your age and musical background, a coach may either choose it for you or with you or make suggestions. As you progress in your free skating, you will learn to keep your ears tuned for music that is appealing to you—and that might be just right for skating. It's a good idea to keep a notebook in which you can write down titles, names of composers, and names of musicians or orchestras. Many skaters choose musical scores from movies, stage shows, or television programs, but these tend to become overused. If your local library has a good selection of records, you may be able to find something suitable there. Listen to different kinds of music and think about how you might be skating to them.

A skating program should have a change in tempo. Although for most programs this is from *fast* to *slow* and then back to *fast*, it can vary. One way to find musical selections that sound well with each other is to assemble them from the same album or from works by the same composer. Have your selections put on a record or tape for your program by a professional who can make smooth blends that will not jar your audience or your judges. It is a good idea to have two copies of your program since music is often mislaid during the excitement of competition.

Once you have your music, your next step will be to plan the moves you are going to do. You and your coach should list the moves you do well. Unless you are reasonably sure you can perfect them in time for the competition, do not include any that you are now learning and can't skate consistently well as yet. Generally speaking, moves should not be repeated except in different combinations. If you do two lutz jumps, for example, you will not get full credit for the second unless you do it—say—followed by a toe loop, without changing feet.

Your program should be balanced. The placing of your moves will be suggested by the highlights of your music, and these highlights should be skated in different parts of the rink (away from the boards) and in different parts of your program. You don't want all your good moves in the beginning, and you should present a variety of moves that includes spins as well as jumps with careful footwork in between. The various moves you can do to connect your spins and jumps are called *linking moves*. They are more than just crossovers, and they can help to make your program interesting. A strong ending is important—this is the part that your audiences and your judges will remember best.

Once you have planned the program, you will have to memorize it. You can learn it as you skate it, or it can be drawn on sheets of paper and learned. You will practice it and perfect it during your free skating sessions and lessons, so that your moves are timed to fit the music and your body can express the music comfortably. After a while, you should be able to run through your complete program twice in an hour; then you will know that you have the stamina to skate it through in front of an audience when you may be feeling nervous. Also, you will want to skate once in your costume before you compete, to make sure it permits the freedom of movement you need and looks the way you want it to.

For the day of competition, you may want to make a checklist of things you must remember, such as extra laces, screws and a screwdriver in case a blade becomes loose, *two* copies of your record or tape. Most skaters keep their skates and their costumes with them at all times when they are traveling to a competition. You will find that a system of warm-ups you can do off the ice at a competition is helpful, too. These can keep you limber while you have to wait between your ice warm-up and your turn to skate. Do keep warm while you are waiting. Then, when your name is called out, you can skate out onto the ice with confidence, take a deep breath to drive away the butterflies, and do your *best*.

PAIR SKATING

By far the most physically demanding branch of figure skating is pair skating. This is actually free skating performed by two skaters in unison to music of their choice, and it includes all the movements known in single free skating as well as certain typical pair moves such as pair spins, pair spirals, lifts, and partner-assisted jumps. The two skaters do not always perform the same movements. They may separate from time to time, but they must convey the impression of skating as a unit, a genuine *pair,* in contrast to independent single skaters. When single skating movements are included, they are usually done simultaneously in parallel (*shadow* skating) or symmetrically (*mirror* skating).

A pair skating competition is made up of two parts, the short program and a free skating program. Both are skated to music chosen by the two skaters. The short program involves performance of certain required movements such as a double salchow jump, a death spiral, a pair spin, and specified pair lifts. The pair free skating program involves skating of an original program, with marks being awarded for technical merit and for composition and style. Accurate performance in unison by the two skaters is a special consideration in the judging of pair skating.

Selection of the right partner is extremely important in pair skating, and the USFSA *Rulebook* states clearly that marks will be deducted ". . . if there is a serious imbalance in their physical characteristics which would result in an obvious lack of unison . . ." Needless to say, it is also very helpful if the two skaters are well-matched temperamentally.

11

Careers in Ice Skating

Probably the most valuable thing you will get from skating is the chance to have a little fun socializing and get some healthful exercise as you learn a sport that you can enjoy for the rest of your life. We are living in materialistic times, however, and many of you are saying, "That's fine, but is there anything else? What do I get for all the money I put into my skating?"

Well, one thing you can be sure of: you will have gained a certain amount of patience and discipline. Anyone who works seriously at learning to skate knows that it requires time and practice to learn the basic movements. It forces you to develop persistence and patience, qualities you will find useful no matter what you do in life. If, for example, you are applying for a job, always be sure to note on your application that you are an ice skater. Every employer looks

for people who will make stable employees, people who come to work on time, who don't take too much sick leave, who follow orders and get along with others. Chances are good that someone with a hobby of ice skating will be more dependable than someone whose hobby is souped-up cars!

Again, if you are applying for admission to college, be sure to note on your application that you are a skater. College admissions officers are looking for something unusual in each applicant, something that makes an individual stand out from the herd. Even if you have only passed the USFSA Preliminary Test, for example, it will look good to the non-skater. If you are a member of a skating association or club, put this down, too. One of the authors of this book has helped several skaters with admission to college, and the fact that the individual was a skater has sometimes made the difference between acceptance and rejection.

WHAT'S NEXT FOR THE SERIOUS SKATER?

Suppose you reach the point where skating around on Saturday or Sunday afternoon is just not enough. What do you do? From the start of this book, the authors have tried to provide the answers you need. First of all, you might talk to your local rink manager. He will know about any skating clubs that meet at his rink which you might be able to join. Don't hesitate to speak to better skaters whom you see and to ask their advice about lessons, skating clubs, where they skate, and roughly how much it will cost you. You will soon find that good skaters everywhere seem to know each other, and they are glad to give advice to beginners. The skating clubs, of course, are usually interested in new members to help support their club programs.

If you are a very good skater (in speed skating or figure skating), you will probably want to enter competition. This means a very demanding life style and requires almost 100 per cent dedication to your skating progress. Once you have reached a certain level, you will be eligible for advanced coaching, conditioning, training camps, and other opportunities to further improve yourself. You will also have the chance to travel to various competitions with the top skaters, those who appear in World and Olympic competition. Although you will not receive pay for this, your travel expenses and often those for members of your family will be covered. You will also be making contacts that will be very helpful after your competition days are over. Your first move, however, is to join one of the national associations and learn as much as you can about your skating.

For speed skaters, there are two associations in the United States: (1) The United States International Skating Association, Beggs Isle, Oconomowoc, Wisconsin 53066. Write in care of George Howie. The USISA promotes Olympic-style speed skating and sponsors lessons and competitions. It does not publish a magazine available to subscribers, but a bulletin is issued regularly to members. (2) The Amateur Skating Union of the United States, 4423 West Deming Place, Chicago, Illinois 60639, sponsors speed skating competitions and supports the Speedskating Hall of Fame in Newburgh, New York. A quarterly, *The Racing Blade,* is available to members only.

The United States Figure Skating Association, located at 20 First Street, Colorado Springs, Colorado 80906, has several hundred member clubs throughout the United States and can advise you about clubs in your area. It establishes figure skating standards, sponsors tests and competitions at every level, sponsors world and Olympic competition, and also maintains records of all tests and competitions. The USFSA *Rulebook* is available to interested persons, and you may also subscribe to *Skating* magazine for information on equipment (such as figure skates and scribes), current summer skating schools, upcoming competition dates, competition results, and other news of interest to figure skaters. You may also wish to subscribe to *Canadian Skater,* an excellent magazine published by the Canadian Figure Skating Association, 333 River Road, Ottawa, Ontario K1L 8B9.

If you are a hockey player, it will be even easier to capitalize on your good skating. Many colleges, prep schools, and even high schools today have hockey teams—and they are always trying to recruit good players. Athletic scholarships and other types of aid are often available. If you are really first-rate, you may eventually want to consider playing professional hockey. There are also many semi-professional teams, and recent expansion of the National Hockey League has resulted in many teen-agers going directly from high school or prep school to the NHL.

For more information about hockey, skaters should contact the Amateur Hockey Association of the United States, 2997 Broadmoor Valley Road, Colorado Springs, Colorado 80906. With a very large membership, this organization promotes amateur hockey throughout the United States, sponsors hockey clinics, and co-operates in the establishment of hockey leagues. You will also find its magazine, *American Hockey and Arena,* helpful to you with news of amateur hockey, summer camps, equipment, competition, youth hockey, and all kinds of tips for the hockey player. (*Hockey News,* a magazine published by W.C.C. Publishing, Ltd., 1434 St. Catherine Street W., Montreal, Quebec H3G 1R7, covers largely news of professional hockey and is directed more at coaches.)

In addition, beginning skaters may wish to contact the Ice Skating Institute of America (ISIA), at 1000 Skokie Boulevard, Wilmette, Illinois 60091. This organization is sponsored by ice rink operators and managers and by builders and suppliers to the industry. It conducts recreational skating tests in figures, pairs, hockey, dance, and speed skating. Your local rink manager or local pro may be able to give you further information.

ICE SHOWS

One of the more glamorous ways to use your skating is to join one of the touring ice shows. These have provided some World and Olympic figure skating champions with contracts of a million dollars or more in the recent past. Don't forget, however, that for every one of the stars there are dozens of other skaters in each of these shows; only the top-billed skaters need to have been national champions. If you are reasonably attractive and a reasonably good skater, you might well qualify for one of these shows. It is a tiring life in many ways, requiring much travel and often two or three shows in one day—but some of the skaters get really "hooked" on this form of show business and continue on tour year after year, long after there is financial need for them to remain.

COACHING

Local skating clubs are always on the lookout for good professionals (pros) to work with beginning and intermediate skaters. The first requirement, of course, is that he or she be a competent skater and familiar with the demands of testing and competition. Even this is not enough, for many good skaters just don't have the personality and considerable degree of patience needed by a good pro. It is one thing to do something on skates well—it is quite another thing to explain to someone else *how* to do it. Some people can be good teachers and others cannot, and the fact is that many of the best-known pros today were never themselves really top skaters.

These days the real demand for skating pros is in the field of recreational skating. Municipal recreation departments, ice rinks, high schools, prep schools, colleges, and universities often offer skating lessons for beginners. You might really enjoy working with children or with beginning skaters in college. If you are in college, your department of physical education or recreation may be interested in offering classes in skating. Colleges and secondary schools often have skating clubs that need professionals. If you know the fundamentals of skating and have the right personality and interest, it does not take a high level of skating ability to teach beginners well.

If you want to coach hockey, it goes without saying that you will have to be a good hockey player as well as a good skater. Stick-handling is equally important. If you are female, of course, you will find that current equal opportunity regulations are motivating more colleges and universities to sponsor women's hockey—and there is an increasing opportunity for women to enter the coaching field.

NEWS REPORTING AND WRITING

A very limited number of opportunities exist for people interested in reporting skating news. Magazines, newspapers, and television channels cover skating competition of all kinds as part of their usual sports coverage. Skating associations usually have a small paid staff to keep official records and to put out magazines, bulletins, and newsletters. Local skating clubs often publish newsletters covering topics of interest to their members, but this is usually volunteer work by the members themselves. There are, as well, people who write books about skating—but this is almost invariably because of their fondness for the sport rather than a desire to make money!

ICE RINK MANAGEMENT

Last but far from least among the practical careers in skating for you to consider is the management or even ownership of a skating rink.

This requires a real interest in skating, but it does not necessarily require skating ability. What it does demand is a genuine liking for people in general and the considerable patience needed to deal with the public. It is also helpful to know bookkeeping and other business procedures, how to sharpen skates properly, how to operate tape recorders, record players, and PA systems, how to operate (and repair) the Zamboni machine that makes "new ice" several times a day, how to keep the compressors and other mechanical equipment of the rink running, and how to deal with building inspectors, safety inspectors, and other officials. A rink manager does not have an easy job—if your local skating rink has a good one, count your blessings!

Werner Groebli, who was featured in the Ice Follies as "Mr. Frick" in some 15,000 performances over a period of forty years. This is his famous exit. (Courtesy of the Ice Follies)

BIBLIOGRAPHY

Boeckl, Willy. *Willy Boeckl on Figure Skating*. New York: The author, 1937.

Brown, Nigel. *Ice-Skating: a History*. London: Nicholas Kaye, Ltd., 1959.

Button, Richard. *Instant Skating*. New York: Grosset & Dunlap, 1964.

Charlotte (Oelschlagel). *Hippodrome Skating Book*. New York: Hippodrome Skating Club, 1916.

Fassi, Carlo. *Figure Skating with Carlo Fassi*. New York: Charles Scribner's Sons, 1980.

Goodman, Neville and Albert. *Handbook of Fen Skating*. London: Sampson, Low, Marston, Searle and Rivington, 1882.

Heathcote, J. M., et al. *Skating—The Badminton Library*. London: Longmans, Green & Co., 1892.

Jeremiah, Eddie. *Ice Hockey*. 2nd ed. New York: Ronald Press Co., 1958.

Ogilvie, Robert S. *Basic Ice Skating Skills*. Philadelphia: J. H. Lippincott Co., 1968.

Owen, Maribel Vinson. *The Fun of Figure Skating*. New York: Harper & Row, 1960.

Percival, Lloyd. *The Hockey Handbook*. Vancouver, B.C., Canada: Copp Clark Publishing Co., Ltd., 1957.

United States Figure Skating Association. *Rulebook 1980–81*. USFSA, 20 First Street, Colorado Springs, CO. 80906.

Vinson, Maribel Y. *Advanced Figure Skating*. New York: Whittlesey House, 1940.

———. *Primer of Figure Skating*. New York: Whittlesey House, 1938.

Wickers, J. Van Buttingha. *Schaatsenrijden*. W. Cremer, 'S-Gravenhage, 1888.